Editors

Mary S. Jones, M.A.

Cristina Krysinski, M. Ed.

Editor in Chief

Karen J. Goldfluss, M.S. Ed.

Creative Director

Sarah M. Smith

Cover Artist

Diem Pascarella

Art Coordinator

Renée McElwee

Imaging

Leonard P. Swierski

Publisher

Mary D. Smith, M.S. Ed.

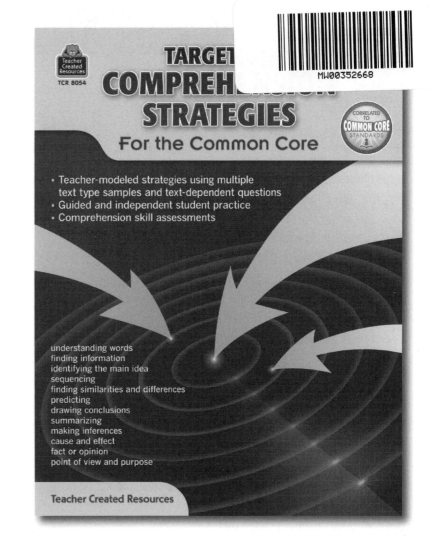

The lessons and activities in each unit have been correlated to Common Core State Standards for English Language Arts. Correlations charts are provided on pages 7 and 8 and can also be found at *http://www.teachercreated.com/standards*.

Teacher Created Resources

6421 Industry Way

Westminster, CA 92683

www.teachercreated.com

ISBN: 978-1-4206-8054-6

© 2014 Teacher Created Resources

Made in U.S.A.

Table of Contents

What Is Comprehension?

Comprehension is a cognitive process. It involves the capacity of the mind to understand, using logic and reasoning. For students, it should be more than a process of trying to guess the answers to formal exercises after reading text. Students need to know **how to think about and make decisions about a text before, during, and after reading it**.

Teaching Comprehension

Comprehension skills can and should be developed by teaching students strategies that are appropriate to a particular comprehension skill and then providing opportunities for them to discuss and practice applying those strategies to the texts they read. These strategies can be a series of clearly defined steps to follow.

Students need to understand that it is the **process**—not the product—that is more important. In other words, they need to understand how it is done before they are required to demonstrate that they can do it.

Higher-order comprehension skills are within the capacity of young students, but care needs to be taken to ensure that the level and language of the text is appropriately assigned.

The text can be read to the students. When introducing comprehension strategies to students, the emphasis should be on the discussion, and the comprehension activities should be completed orally before moving on to supported and then independent practice and application. The lessons in this book are scaffolded to accommodate this process.

Note: Some students may not be able to complete the activities independently. For those students, additional support should be provided as they work through the activities within each unit.

Before students start the activities in this book, discuss the concepts of paragraphs and stanzas. Note that the paragraphs in each reading passage or stanza have been numbered for easy reference as students complete activities.

The terms *skills* and *strategies* are sometimes confused. The following explanation provides some clarification of how the two terms are used in this book.

Skills relate to competent performance and come from knowledge, practice, and aptitude.

Strategies involve planning and tactics.

In other words, we can teach *strategies* that will help students acquire specific comprehension *skills*.

Twelve comprehension skills are introduced in this book. Information about these skills and how the units and lessons are designed to explore them are provided on pages 4 – 6.

Metacognitive Strategies

Metacognitive strategies, which involve teaching students how to think about thinking, are utilized in developing the twelve comprehension skills taught in this book. Metacognitive strategies are modeled and explained to students for each skill. As this is essentially an oral process, teachers are encouraged to elaborate on and discuss the explanations provided on each "Learning Page." The activities on these pages allow students to talk about the different thought processes they would use in answering each question.

Students will require different levels of support before they are able to work independently to comprehend, make decisions about text, and choose the best answer in multiple-choice questions. This support is provided within each unit lesson by including guided practice, modeled practice using the metacognitive processes, and assisted practice using hints and clues.

Comprehension Strategies

The exercises in this book have been written—not to test—but to stimulate and challenge students and to help them develop their thinking processes through modeled metacognitive strategies, discussion, and guided and independent practice. There are no trick questions, but many require and encourage students to use logic and reasoning.

Particularly in the higher-order comprehension skills, there may be more than one acceptable answer. The reader's prior knowledge and experience will influence some of his or her decisions about the text. Teachers may choose to accept an answer if a student can justify and explain his or her choice. Therefore, some of the answers provided should not be considered prescriptive but more of a guide and a basis for discussion.

Some students with excellent cognitive processing skills, who have a particular aptitude for and acquire an interest in reading, tend to develop advanced reading comprehension skills independently. However, for the majority of students, the strategies they need to develop and demonstrate comprehension need to be made explicit and carefully guided, not just tested, which is the rationale behind this series of books.

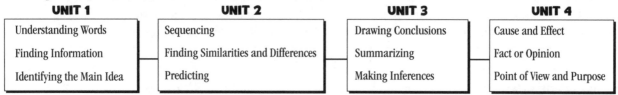

The following twelve comprehension skills are included in this book. Strategies for improving these skills are provided through sets of lessons for each of the skills. These twelve skills have been divided into four units, each with teachers' notes and answer keys, three different comprehension skills, and three student assessment tests.

UNIT 1	UNIT 2	UNIT 3	UNIT 4
Understanding Words	Sequencing	Drawing Conclusions	Cause and Effect
Finding Information	Finding Similarities and Differences	Summarizing	Fact or Opinion
Identifying the Main Idea	Predicting	Making Inferences	Point of View and Purpose

Each skill listed above has a six-page lesson to help students build stronger comprehension skills in that area by using specific strategies.

- Text 1 (first reading text page for use with practice pages)
- Learning Page (learning about the skill with teacher modeling)
- Practice Page (student practice with teacher assistance)
- On Your Own (independent student activity)
- Text 2 (second reading text page for use with practice page)
- Try It Out (independent student activity with one clue)

A test at the end of each unit assesses the three skills taught in the unit. The assessment section includes:

- Assessment Text (reading text used for all three assessments)
- Assessment test for the first skill in the unit
- Assessment test for the second skill in the unit
- Assessment test for the third skill in the unit

 Included in this book is a CD containing reproducible, PDF-formatted files for all activity pages, as well as Common Core State Standards. The PDF files are ideal for group instruction using interactive whiteboards.

Text Types

In addition to applying comprehension strategies to better understand content, students will experience reading and interpreting a variety of text types.

- Reports
- Narratives
- Expositions
- Recounts
- Procedures
- Explanations

Teacher and Student Pages

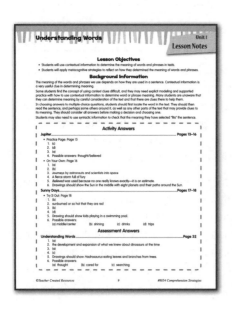

Lesson Notes

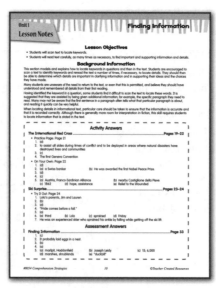

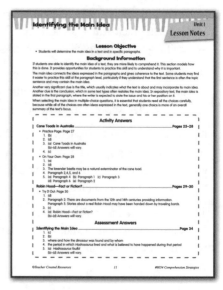

Each of the four units contains lessons that address three specific comprehension skills. Every Lesson Notes page includes:

- Lesson objective indicators state expected outcomes.

- Background information about the skill and teaching strategies.

- An answer key for student pages and assessment pages. (*Note:* Answers may vary, particularly with higher-order comprehension skills. Teachers may choose to accept alternative answers if students are able to justify their responses.)

Helpful Hints

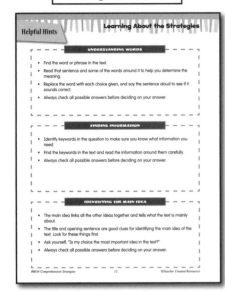

- All three comprehension skills for the unit are identified. These serve as reminders for students as they complete the activities.
- Helpful hints are provided for each skill in bullet-point form.

Text 1

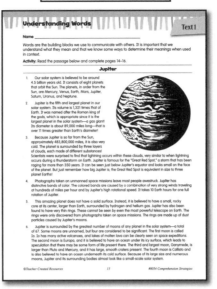

- The skill is identified and defined.
- The text is presented to students using oral, silent, partner, or read-aloud methods. Choose a technique or approach most suitable to your classroom needs.

Learning Page

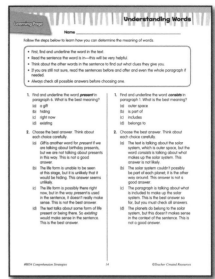

- This is a teacher-student interaction page.
- Steps and strategies are outlined, discussed, and referenced using the text page.
- Multiple-choice questions are presented, and metacognitive processes for choosing the best answer are described.

Practice Page

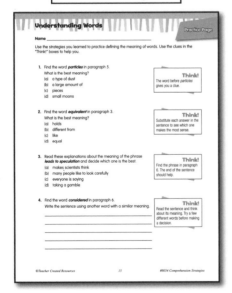

- Using the text page content, students practice strategies to complete the questions. The teacher provides guidance as needed.
- Some multiple-choice questions and others requiring explanations are presented with prompts or clues to assist students.

On Your Own

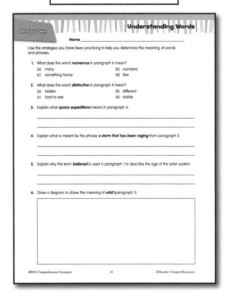

- This page is completed independently.
- At least one multiple-choice question and others requiring explanations are presented for students to complete.

Text 2

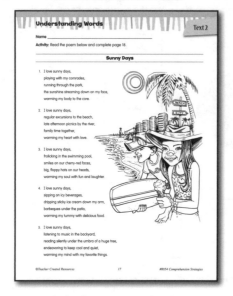

- As with the first text page for the lesson, the skill is identified.
- Presentation of the text is decided by the teacher.

Try It Out

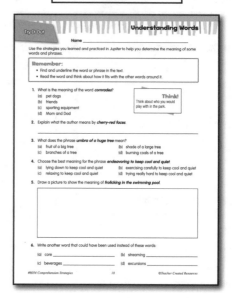

- This page can be completed independently by the student.
- Multiple-choice questions and some requiring explanation are included.

Assessment Text

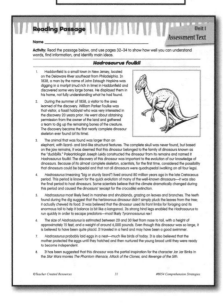

- The three skills to be tested are identified.
- The assessment text is presented.

Unit Assessments

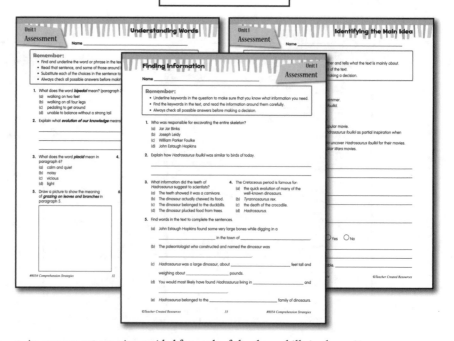

- An assessment page is provided for each of the three skills in the unit.
- The comprehension skill to be tested is identified and students apply their knowledge and strategies to complete each page, using the content of the Assessment Text page.
- Multiple-choice questions and others requiring more explanation are presented.

Common Core State Standards Correlations

Each lesson meets one or more of the following Common Core State Standards © Copyright 2010. National Governors Association Center for Best Practices and Council of Chief State School Officers. All rights reserved. For more information about the Common Core State Standards, go to *http://www.corestandards.org/* or *htp://www.teachercreated.com/standards*.

READING: LITERATURE STANDARDS	Pages
Key Ideas and Details	
ELA.RL.7.1: Cite several pieces of textual evidence to support analysis of what the text says explicitly as well as inferences drawn from the text.	17-18, 23-24, 39-42, 51-54, 55-56, 57-60, 69-70, 77-80, 81-82
ELA.RL.7.2: Determine a theme or central idea of a text and analyze its development over the course of the text; provide an objective summary of the text.	23-24, 39-42, 49-50, 51-54, 55-56, 57-60, 77-80, 97-100, 103-106, 107-108
ELA.RL.7.3: Analyze how particular elements of a story or drama interact (e.g., how setting shapes the characters or plot).	23-24, 39-42, 49-50, 51-54, 57-60, 69-70
Craft and Structure	
ELA.RL.7.4: Determine the meaning of words and phrases as they are used in a text, including figurative and connotative meanings; analyze the impact of rhymes and other repetitions of sounds (e.g., alliteration) on a specific verse or stanza of a poem or section of a story or drama.	17-18, 23-24, 39-42, 49-50, 51-54, 55-56, 57-60, 69-70, 77-80, 81-82, 97-100, 103-106, 107-108
ELA.RL.7.6: Analyze how an author develops and contrasts the points of view of different characters or narrators in a text.	97-100, 103-106, 107-108
Range of Reading and Level of Text Complexity	
ELA.RL.7.10: By the end of the year, read and comprehend literature, including stories, dramas, and poems, in the grades 6–8 text complexity band proficiently, with scaffolding as needed at the high end of the range.	All passages allow students to read and comprehend literature in the grades 6-8 text complexity band.

READING: INFORMATIONAL TEXT STANDARDS	Pages
Key Ideas and Details	
ELA.RI.7.1: Cite several pieces of textual evidence to support analysis of what the text says explicitly as well as inferences drawn from the text.	13-16, 19-22, 25-28, 29-30, 31-34, 43-44, 45-48, 65-68, 71-74, 83-86, 91-94
ELA.RI.7.2: Determine two or more central ideas in a text and analyze their development over the course of the text; provide an objective summary of the text.	13-16, 19-22, 25-28, 31-34, 65-68, 71-74, 75-76, 83-86, 91-94, 101-102, 109-112
ELA.RI.7.3: Analyze the interactions between individuals, events, and ideas in a text (e.g., how ideas influence individuals or events, or how individuals influence ideas or events).	25-28, 31-34, 45-48, 65-68, 71-74, 75-76, 83-86, 91-94, 95-96, 101-102, 109-112
Craft and Structure	
ELA.RI.7.4: Determine the meaning of words and phrases as they are used in a text, including figurative, connotative, and technical meanings; analyze the impact of a specific word choice on meaning and tone.	13-16, 19-22, 25-28, 29-30, 31-34, 43-44, 45-48, 65-68, 71-74, 75-76, 83-86, 91-94, 95-96, 101-102, 109-112
ELA.RI.7.6: Determine an author's point of view or purpose in a text and analyze how the author distinguishes his or her position from that of others.	101-102, 109-112
Integration of Knowledge and Ideas	
ELA.RI.7.8: Trace and evaluate the argument and specific claims in a text, assessing whether the reasoning is sound and the evidence is relevant and sufficient to support the claims.	91-94, 95-96, 101-102, 109-112
Range of Reading and Level of Text Complexity	
ELA.RI.7.10: By the end of the year, read and comprehend literary nonfiction in the grades 6–8 text complexity band proficiently, with scaffolding as needed at the high end of the range.	All passages allow students to read and comprehend literary nonfiction in the grades 6-8 text complexity band.

Lesson Objectives

- Students will use contextual information to determine the meaning of words and phrases in texts.
- Students will apply metacognitive strategies to reflect on how they determined the meaning of words and phrases.

Background Information

The meaning of the words and phrases we use depends on how they are used in a sentence. Contextual information is a very useful clue in determining meaning.

Some students find the concept of using context clues difficult, and they may need explicit modeling and supported practice with how to use contextual information to determine word or phrase meaning. Many students are unaware that they can determine meaning by careful consideration of the text and that there are clues there to help them.

In choosing answers to multiple-choice questions, students should first locate the word in the text. They should then read the sentence, and perhaps some others around it, as well as any other parts of the text that may provide clues to its meaning. They should consider all answers before making a decision and choosing one.

Students may also need to use syntactic information to check that the meaning they have selected "fits" the sentence.

Activity Answers

Jupiter..**Pages 13–16**

- Practice Page: Page 15
  1. (c)
  2. (d)
  3. (a)
  4. Possible answers: thought/believed

- On Your Own: Page 16
  1. (a)
  2. (b)
  3. Journeys by astronauts and scientists into space
  4. A fierce storm full of fury
  5. *Believed* was used because no one really knows exactly—it is an estimate.
  6. Drawings should show the Sun in the middle with eight planets and their paths around the Sun.

Sunny Days..**Pages 17–18**

- Try It Out: Page 18
  1. (b)
  2. sunburned or so hot that they are red
  3. (b)
  4. (d)
  5. Drawing should show kids playing in a swimming pool.
  6. Possible answers:
     (a) middle/center (b) shining (c) drinks (d) trips

Assessment Answers

Understanding Words...**Page 32**

1. (a)
2. the development and expansion of what we knew about dinosaurs at the time
3. (a)
4. (c)
5. Drawings should show *Hadrosaurus* eating leaves and branches from trees.
6. Possible answers:
   (a) thought (b) cared for (c) searching

Lesson Objectives

- Students will scan text to locate keywords.
- Students will read text carefully, as many times as necessary, to find important and supporting information and details.

Background Information

This section models and explains how to locate keywords in questions and then in the text. Students are encouraged to scan a text to identify keywords and reread the text a number of times, if necessary, to locate details. They should then be able to determine which details are important in clarifying information and in supporting their ideas and the choices they have made.

Many students are unaware of the need to return to the text, or even that this is permitted, and believe they should have understood and remembered all details from their first reading.

Having identified the keyword in a question, some students find it difficult to scan the text to locate these words. It is suggested that they are assisted by being given additional information; for example, the specific paragraph they need to read. Many may not be aware that the first sentence in a paragraph often tells what that particular paragraph is about, and reading it quickly can be very helpful.

When locating details in informational text, particular care should be taken to ensure that the information is accurate and that it is recorded correctly. Although there is generally more room for interpretation in fiction, this skill requires students to locate information that is stated in the text.

Activity Answers

The International Red Cross ....**Pages 19–22**

- Practice Page: Page 21
  1. (d)
  2. to assist all sides during times of conflict and to be deployed in areas where natural disasters have destroyed lives and communities
  3. (c)
  4. The first Geneva Convention
- On Your Own: Page 22
  1. (d)
  2. (a) a Swiss banker   (b) He was awarded the first Nobel Peace Prize.
  3. (d)
  4. (c)
  5. (a) Austria, Franco-Sardinian Alliance   (b) nearby Castiglione della Pieve
     (c) 1862   (d) hope, assistance   (e) Relief to the Wounded

Ski Surprise...**Pages 23–24**

- Try It Out: Page 24
  1. Lola's parents, Jim and Lauren
  2. (b)
  3. (d)
  4. "Pride comes before a fall."
  5. (a)
  6. (a) third   (b) Lola   (c) sprained   (d) Friday
  7. He was an experienced skier who sprained his ankle by falling while getting off the ski lift.

Assessment Answers

Finding Information ....**Page 33**
  1. (c)
  2. It probably laid eggs in a nest.
  3. (b)
  4. (a)
  5. (a) marlpit, Haddonfield   (b) Joseph Leidy   (c) 15; 6,000
     (d) marshes, shrublands   (e) "duckbill"

Lesson Objective

- Students will determine the main idea in a text and in specific paragraphs.

Background Information

If students are able to identify the main idea of a text, they are more likely to comprehend it. This section models how this is done. It provides opportunities for students to practice this skill and to understand why it is important.

The main idea connects the ideas expressed in the paragraphs and gives coherence to the text. Some students may find it easier to practice this skill at the paragraph level, particularly if they understand that the first sentence is often the topic sentence and may contain the main idea.

Another very significant clue is the title, which usually indicates what the text is about and may incorporate its main idea. Another clue is the conclusion, which in some text types often restates the main idea. In expository text, the main idea is stated in the first paragraph, where the writer is expected to state the issue and his or her position on it.

When selecting the main idea in multiple-choice questions, it is essential that students read all the choices carefully, because while all of the choices are often ideas expressed in the text, generally one choice is more of an overall summary of the text's focus.

Activity Answers

Cane Toads in Australia ....**Pages 25–28**

- Practice Page: Page 27
  1. (b)
  2. (d)
  3. (a) Cane Toads in Australia
     (b)–(d) Answers will vary.
  4. (c)

- On Your Own: Page 28
  1. (a)
  2. (d)
  3. The lavender beetle may be a natural exterminator of the cane toad.
  4. Paragraph 2,4,5, and 6
  5. (a) Paragraph 4 (b) Paragraph 1 (c) Paragraph 3
     (d) Paragraph 6 (e) Paragraph 2

Robin Hood—Fact or Fiction? ....**Pages 29–30**

- Try It Out: Page 30
  1. (d)
  2. Paragraph 2: There are documents from the 12th and 14th centuries providing information.
     Paragraph 5: Stories about a real Robin Hood may have been handed down by traveling bards.
  3. (c)
  4. (a) Robin Hood—Fact or Fiction?
     (b)–(d) Answers will vary.

Assessment Answers

Identifying the Main Idea ....**Page 34**
  1. (c)
  2. (b)
  3. where and how the dinosaur was found and by whom
  4. the period in which *Hadrosaurus* lived and what is believed to have happened during that period
  5. (a) *Hadrosaurus foulkii*
     (b)–(d) Answers will vary.

UNDERSTANDING WORDS

- Find the word or phrase in the text.

- Read that sentence and some of the words around it to help you determine the meaning.

- Replace the word with each choice given, and say the sentence aloud to see if it sounds correct.

- Always check all possible answers before deciding on your answer.

FINDING INFORMATION

- Identify keywords in the question to make sure you know what information you need.

- Find the keywords in the text and read the information around them carefully.

- Always check all possible answers before deciding on your answer.

IDENTIFYING THE MAIN IDEA

- The main idea links all the other ideas together and tells what the text is mainly about.

- The title and opening sentence are good clues for identifying the main idea of the text. Look for these things first.

- Ask yourself, "Is my choice the most important idea in the text?"

- Always check all possible answers before deciding on your answer.

Understanding Words

Name _____

Words are the building blocks we use to communicate with others. It is important that we understand what they mean and that we know some ways to determine their meanings when used in context.

Activity: Read the passage below and complete pages 14–16.

Jupiter

1.   Our solar system is believed to be around 4.5 billion years old. It consists of eight planets that orbit the Sun. The planets, in order from the Sun, are Mercury, Venus, Earth, Mars, Jupiter, Saturn, Uranus, and Neptune.

2.   Jupiter is the fifth and largest planet in our solar system. Its volume is 1,321 times that of Earth. It was named after the Roman king of the gods, which is appropriate since it is the largest planet in the solar system—a gas giant! Its diameter is about 89,000 miles long—that is over 11 times greater than Earth's diameter!

3.   Because Jupiter is so far from the Sun, approximately 483,800,000 miles, it is also very cold. The planet is surrounded by three layers of clouds, each made of different substances! Scientists were surprised to find that lightning occurs within these clouds, very similar to when lightning occurs during a thunderstorm on Earth. Jupiter is famous for the "Great Red Spot," a storm that has been raging for more than 350 years. It can be seen just below Jupiter's equator and looks small on the face of the planet. But just remember how big Jupiter is; the Great Red Spot is equivalent in size to three planet Earths!

4.   Photographs taken on unmanned space missions leave most people awestruck. Jupiter has distinctive bands of color. The colored bands are caused by a combination of very strong winds traveling at hundreds of miles per hour and by Jupiter's high rotational speed. It takes 10 Earth hours for one full rotation of Jupiter.

5.   This amazing planet does not have a solid surface. Instead, it is believed to have a small, rocky core at its center, larger than Earth, surrounded by hydrogen and helium gas. Jupiter has also been found to have very thin rings. These cannot be seen by even the most powerful telescope on Earth. The rings were only discovered from photographs taken on space missions. The rings are made up of dust particles caused by Jupiter's moons.

6.   Jupiter is surrounded by the greatest number of moons of any planet in the solar system—a total of 67. Some moons are unnamed, but four are considered to be significant. The first moon is called Io. Io has many active volcanoes, and lakes of molten lava can be clearly seen on space expeditions. The second moon is Europa, and it is believed to have an ocean under its icy surface, which leads to speculation that there may be some form of life present there. The third and largest moon, Ganymede, is larger than Pluto and Mercury, and it has large, smooth craters present. The fourth moon is Callisto and is also believed to have an ocean underneath its cold surface. Because of its large size and numerous moons, Jupiter and its surrounding bodies almost look like a small-scale solar system.

Name _____

Follow the steps below to learn how you can determine the meaning of words.

- First, find and underline the word in the text.
- Read the sentence the word is in—this will be very helpful.
- Think about the other words in the sentence to find out what clues they give you.
- If you are still not sure, read the sentences before and after and even the whole paragraph if needed.
- Always check all possible answers before choosing one.

1. Find and underline the word **present** in paragraph 6. What is the best meaning?

   (a) a gift
   (b) hiding
   (c) right now
   (d) existing

2. Choose the best answer. Think about each choice carefully.

   (a) *Gift* is another word for *present* if we are talking about birthday presents, but we are not talking about presents in this way. This is not a good answer.

   (b) The life form is unable to be seen at this stage, but it is unlikely that it would be hiding. This answer seems unlikely.

   (c) The life form is possibly there right now, but in the way *present* is used in the sentence, it doesn't really make sense. This is not the best answer.

   (d) The text talks about some form of life present or being there. So *existing* would make sense in the sentence. This is the best answer.

1. Find and underline the word **consists** in paragraph 1. What is the best meaning?

   (a) outer space
   (b) is part of
   (c) includes
   (d) belongs to

2. Choose the best answer. Think about each choice carefully.

   (a) The text is talking about the solar system, which is outer space, but the word *consists* is talking about what makes up the solar system. This answer is not likely.

   (b) The solar system couldn't possibly be part of each planet; it is the other way around. This answer is not a good answer.

   (c) The paragraph is talking about what is included to make up the solar system. This is the best answer so far, but you must check all answers.

   (d) The planets do belong to the solar system, but this doesn't makes sense in the context of the sentence. This is not a good answer.

Name _____

Use the strategies you learned to practice defining the meaning of words. Use the clues in the "Think!" boxes to help you.

1. Find the word **particles** in paragraph 5.

   What is the best meaning?

   (a)   a type of dust

   (b)   a large amount of

   (c)   pieces

   (d)   small moons

   > **Think!**
   > The word before *particles* gives you a clue.

2. Find the word **equivalent** in paragraph 3.

   What is the best meaning?

   (a)   holds

   (b)   different from

   (c)   like

   (d)   equal

   > **Think!**
   > Substitute each answer in the sentence to see which one makes the most sense.

3. Read these explanations about the meaning of the phrase **leads to speculation** and decide which one is the best.

   (a)   makes scientists think

   (b)   many people like to look carefully

   (c)   everyone is saying

   (d)   taking a gamble

   > **Think!**
   > Find the phrase in paragraph 6. The end of the sentence should help.

4. Find the word **considered** in paragraph 6.

   Write the sentence using another word with a similar meaning.

   "... but four are ~~thought~~ to be significant."

   _____

   _____

   _____

   > **Think!**
   > Read the sentence and think about its meaning. Try a few different words before making a decision.

Name _____

Use the strategies you have been practicing to help you determine the meaning of words and phrases.

1. What does the word **numerous** in paragraph 6 mean?

   (a) many   (b) numbers

   (c) something funny   (d) few

2. What does the word **distinctive** in paragraph 4 mean?

   (a) hidden   (b) different

   (c) hard to see   (d) visible

3. Explain what **space expeditions** means in paragraph 6.

   _____

   _____

4. Explain what is meant by the phrase **a storm that has been raging** from paragraph 3.

   It means that the storm has been raging
   for awhile.

5. Explain why the term **believed** is used in paragraph 1 to describe the age of the solar system.

   _____

   _____

6. Draw a diagram to show the meaning of **orbit** (paragraph 1).

   _____

Understanding Words

Name _____

Activity: Read the poem below and complete page 18.

Sunny Days

1. I love sunny days,
   playing with my comrades,
   running through the park,
   the sunshine streaming down on my face,
   warming my body to the core.

2. I love sunny days,
   regular excursions to the beach,
   late afternoon picnics by the river,
   family time together,
   warming my heart with love.

3. I love sunny days,
   frolicking in the swimming pool,
   smiles on our cherry-red faces,
   big, floppy hats on our heads,
   warming my soul with fun and laughter.

4. I love sunny days,
   sipping on icy beverages,
   dripping sticky ice cream down my arm,
   barbeques under the patio,
   warming my tummy with delicious food.

5. I love sunny days,
   listening to music in the backyard,
   reading silently under the umbra of a huge tree,
   endeavoring to keep cool and quiet,
   warming my mind with my favorite things.

Name _____

Use the strategies you learned and practiced in *Jupiter* to help you determine the meaning of some words and phrases.

> ## Remember:
> - Find and underline the word or phrase in the text.
> - Read the word and think about how it fits with the other words around it.

1. What is the meaning of the word ***comrades***?

(a) pet dogs

(b) friends

(c) sporting equipment

(d) Mom and Dad

> ## Think!
> Think about who you would play with in the park.

2. Explain what the author means by ***cherry-red faces***.

_____

3. What does the phrase ***umbra of a huge tree*** mean?

(a) fruit of a big tree   (b) shade of a large tree

(c) branches of a tree   (d) burning coals of a tree

4. Choose the best meaning for the phrase ***endeavoring to keep cool and quiet***.

(a) lying down to keep cool and quiet   (b) exercising carefully to keep cool and quiet

(c) relaxing to keep cool and quiet   (d) trying really hard to keep cool and quiet

5. Draw a picture to show the meaning of ***frolicking in the swimming pool***.

6. Write another word that could have been used instead of these words:

(a) core _____   (b) streaming _____

(c) beverages _____   (d) excursions _____

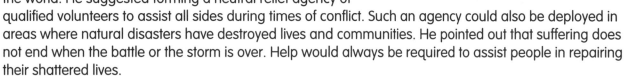

Name _____

When you read text, you can usually remember some information. If you are asked about details, you should refer back to the text to locate your information and check that it is correct. Remember, the answer you are looking for is there in the text—you just need to find it.

Activity: Read the passage below and complete pages 20–22.

The International Red Cross

1. When traveling in northern Italy during the hot summer of 1859, a Swiss banker named Henry Dunant witnessed such a horrifying sight that he was inspired to establish the organization that we know today as the Red Cross.

2. The Battle of Solferino between Austria and the Franco-Sardinian Alliance had left many men dead, dying, and abandoned. Those barely clinging to life suffered from pain, thirst, searing heat, and flies. Deeply moved by this harrowing scene, Dunant felt great compassion and was compelled to act, urging villagers from nearby Castiglione della Pieve to help care for the injured. In providing this practical support, these people became the first volunteers of the Red Cross.

3. In 1862, Dunant published a book, *A Memory of Solferino*, in which he claimed that all societies have their vulnerable people and that the combined power of humankind could be harnessed to ease the suffering of such people all over the world. He suggested forming a neutral relief agency of qualified volunteers to assist all sides during times of conflict. Such an agency could also be deployed in areas where natural disasters have destroyed lives and communities. He pointed out that suffering does not end when the battle or the storm is over. Help would always be required to assist people in repairing their shattered lives.

4. The International Committee for Relief to the Wounded, later to be known as the International Committee of the Red Cross, was set up in October 1863 under the leadership of Henry Dunant. The committee wanted to guarantee protection for its medical volunteers on the battlefield by having it officially recognized. In answer to their request, the Swiss government invited other nations to attend a diplomatic conference in Geneva in 1864. At that conference, representatives from 12 European countries and the United States of America signed an agreement that was to be the first Geneva Convention, which internationally protects medical volunteers on the battlefield.

5. Since then, a number of changes and developments have occurred within the organization, but the fundamental role of its volunteers has remained the same—to care for people in need regardless of nationality. The emblem chosen by the original committee, a red cross on a white background, is recognized throughout the world as a symbol of hope and assistance. To date, 189 countries have accepted the terms of the Geneva Conventions.

6. In 1901, 42 years after the Battle of Solferino, Henry Dunant was awarded the first Nobel Peace Prize for his role in founding the International Red Cross. Through the tireless efforts of Henry Dunant and the first members of the Red Cross organization, the world has a magnificent relief agency of volunteers who selflessly offer their services in so many ways. They are living proof that the combined power of humankind can indeed be harnessed to ease the suffering of people all over the world.

Name _____

Follow the steps below to learn how to find information in a text.

- Underline the keywords in the question to make sure you know what information is needed.
- Find and underline the keywords in the text, and read the information around them carefully.
- Always check all possible answers before making a decision.

1. What moved Henry Dunant so deeply that he felt compelled to act?

   (a) The dead and injured attracted flies and disease.

   (b) Looters were stealing from the dead and injured.

   (c) No one was burying the dead.

   (d) So many abandoned men suffered from pain, thirst, searing heat, and flies.

2. Choose the best answer. Think about each choice carefully.

   (a) Although the scene would attract flies and eventually disease, the text does not give this as a reason for Dunant's feelings. This is not a good answer.

   (b) The text does not mention looters, so this is not a good answer.

   (c) The text says that many men were dead, but Dunant was more interested in helping and caring for the injured. This is not the best answer.

   (d) This describes the scene that deeply moved Dunant, compelling him to act. This is the best answer.

1. What did Dunant mean when he said that *suffering does not end when the battle or the storm is over*? (paragraph 3)

   (a) Enemies still dislike one another.

   (b) There will always be wars and destructive natural forces.

   (c) People are still upset even after the war or disaster.

   (d) People need assistance to rebuild their shattered lives after a war or a disaster.

2. Choose the best answer. Think about each choice carefully.

   (a) This may be so, but it is not mentioned in the text. This is not a good answer.

   (b) This is probably true, but it is not mentioned in the text. This is not a good answer.

   (c) This is definitely true, but it is too general, and it is not mentioned in the text. This is not a good answer.

   (d) The sentence after this phrase says that help would always be required to assist these people. This is the best answer.

Finding Information

Name _____

Use the strategies you learned to practice finding information. Use the clues in the "Think!" boxes to help you.

1. What did Dunant claim about mankind in *A Memory of Solferino*?

   (a)   All people are vulnerable.

   (b)   It would be easy to help suffering people all over the world.

   (c)   There are people willing to help in all societies.

   (d)   The power of humankind could be used to ease suffering in the world.

> **Think!**
> Find the title of the book in paragraph 3, and read on to find what he claimed.

2. What were Dunant's two key roles for a neutral relief agency?

   • _____

     _____

     _____

   • _____

     _____

     _____

> **Think!**
> Find the words **neutral relief agency** in paragraph 3 and read on to find what he wanted it to do.

3. Having established the International Committee for Relief to the Wounded, why did Dunant want it officially recognized?

   (a)   He wanted the world to know what a great idea it was.

   (b)   He wanted the name changed to the Red Cross.

   (c)   He wanted to ensure protection for its medical volunteers on the battlefield.

   (d)   He wanted other countries to be involved.

> **Think!**
> Find the words **officially recognized** in paragraph 4, and read the whole sentence.

4. What was the outcome of the diplomatic conference held in Geneva in 1864?

_____

_____

_____

> **Think!**
> Underline the keywords in paragraph 4. Read the whole sentence and the one following.

Finding Information

Name _____

Use the strategies you have been practicing to help you find information in the text.

1. What is the fundamental role of Red Cross volunteers?
   - (a) to give money to the organization
   - (b) to be prepared to travel immediately to a stricken area
   - (c) to make developmental changes in the organization
   - (d) to care for people in need regardless of their nationality

2. (a) Who was Henry Dunant? _____

   (b) How was he recognized in 1901 for helping others? _____

   _____

3. About how many years after the Battle of Solferino was the International Committee of the Red Cross set up?
   - (a) 10 years
   - (b) 15 years
   - (c) 1 year
   - (d) 4 years

4. Which word best describes how Henry Dunant felt when he was compelled to act?
   - (a) energetic
   - (b) assertive
   - (c) compassionate
   - (d) kind

5. Find words in the text to complete the sentences.
   - (a) The Battle of Solferino was fought between _____ and the

     _____.

   - (b) Villagers from _____ became
     the first volunteers of the Red Cross.

   - (c) Dunant's book, *A Memory of Solferino*, was published in _____.

   - (d) The emblem of the Red Cross is a symbol of _____ and

     _____.

   - (e) The International Committee of the Red Cross was previously known as the

     International Committee for _____.

Finding Information

Name _____

Activity: Read the story below and complete page 24.

Ski Surprise

1.   Jenna and her parents were about to embark on their first ski trip with Lola, Jenna's best friend, and Lola's parents. The girls were wild with excitement, but Jenna's parents, Bob and Lou, were a little less enthusiastic.

2.   "Don't worry," soothed Lauren, Lola's mom. "By the third day of ski lessons, you'll be flying!"

3.   "That's what I'm afraid of!" muttered Bob as he wondered, not for the first time, why he had agreed to Jim and Lauren's ridiculous idea for a vacation.

4.   After they had settled into their roomy cabin, they had just enough time to rent skis, poles, and boots, sign up for ski lessons, and buy their lift tickets before darkness fell.

5.   At lunchtime the next day, the girls and Jenna's parents met to share stories about their first morning in ski lessons. Jim and Lauren, who were experienced skiers, were on the higher slopes and would not return before late afternoon.

6.   "What a laugh!" cried Bob, as he told the others how Lou had spent most of the morning lying on the ground like an upturned insect, trying unsuccessfully to regain her position and her composure.

7.   "Okay, so I wasn't as good as you, Mr. Teacher's Pet," retorted Lou huffily. "But just remember your Grandma's old saying, 'Pride comes before a fall.'"

8.   As Lauren had predicted, by the third day, the four novices were feeling very comfortable on the slopes and enjoying the freedom of practicing their newly acquired skills each afternoon.

9.   "It's so exhilarating!" sighed Lola. "Feeling the cold, crisp air bite your face as you whoosh down the hillside… I can't wait for the race on Friday."

10.   "Just you be careful, young lady," Jim warned his daughter. "Don't get carried away in that race. That's how legs get broken." Lola's parents had been skiing many times before, so Lola heeded her father's advice. But the following day proved otherwise…

11.   "What a way to end a vacation!" sobbed Lola.

12.   "Cheer up, Lola," comforted her friend. "It could have been worse. The doctor said his ankle wasn't broken, just badly sprained."

13.   "Oh, it's broken all right—his pride, I mean," explained Lola. "Dad'll never live down the shame of all of us doing so well in our races and him falling while getting off the ski lift."

14.   "That's true, sweetheart," whispered her mom, "but I managed to capture the moment, and it's a classic. Shall we stick the photo on the fridge?"

Name _____

Use the strategies you learned and practiced in *The International Red Cross* to help you find information.

> **Remember:**
> - Determine the keywords and find them in the text.
> - Check all answers before you make a decision.

1. Who suggested going on a ski trip?

> **Think!**
> Read paragraph 3.

_____

2. How were Jenna's parents feeling about the trip in the beginning?

    (a)   excited   (b)   hesitant

    (c)   thrilled   (d)   eager

3. When did the girls and Jenna's parents meet up to discuss their first ski lesson?

    (a)   in the morning   (b)   after dark

    (c)   dinnertime   (d)   lunchtime

4. What was Bob's grandma's old saying?

_____

5. Who was described as *an upturned insect*?

    (a)   Lou   (b) Bob

    (c)   Jenna   (d) Jim

6. Find words in the text to complete the sentences.

    (a)   The four novices were feeling comfortable on the slopes by the _____ day.

    (b)   "What a way to end a vacation!" was said by _____.

    (c)   Jim's ankle was _____ but not broken.

    (d)   The ski race they competed in was held on _____.

7. Explain why Jim would return home feeling ashamed.

_____

_____

Identifying the Main Idea

Name _____

If you know the main idea of a text, you will have a much better chance of understanding what the content is about.

Activity: Read the passage below and complete pages 26–28.

Cane Toads in Australia

1.   The cane toad was introduced into Australia in 1935. Its mission was to eradicate the cane beetle, which was destroying the sugar crops in northern Queensland. However, it soon became evident that the toads were unable to perform this task and were becoming greater pests themselves.

2.   The cane toad is a deadly amphibian. At all stages of its life, from egg to adult, it is poisonous. An adult oozes poison from the numerous glands on its back and two bulging shoulder sacs. While some animals may have learned to avoid the toad, any that do eat it die very quickly. Even an animal that chooses not to eat the toad, but has used its mouth to investigate it, will still have easily absorbed the poison through its body tissue and be adversely affected by the poison. Kangaroos, snakes, lizards, quolls, dingoes, water fowl, and crocodiles are among the animals falling victim to cane toad poison.

3.   While normally preying on insects, the cane toad will eat anything that will fit into its mouth in an effort to satisfy its hunger. It feasts on small reptiles and mammals, frogs, and birds. The cane toad's poison and appetite has had a devastating impact on the environment. The number of many native species is declining at an alarming rate, and others, such as the threatened Northern quoll, are disappearing completely from areas invaded by the cane toad.

4.   For over 70 years, the cane toad has maintained an invasive attack on the native wildlife population of Australia, establishing itself across great areas of Queensland and the Northern Territory. It is extending its territory each year as numbers continue to rise. The rapid breeding cycle and high number of eggs produced with each spawning has helped the population of the hardy cane toad exceed to 100 million.

5.   Currently, no means of halting the progress of cane toad numbers and migration are effective. Capturing and killing adult toads and collecting and destroying the long, jelly-like strings of eggs from the water would reduce numbers in a local area, but it would have to be an ongoing process with constant monitoring. In remote, inaccessible areas such as Kakadu National Park in the Northern Territory, this would be an impossible task to implement.

6.   There may be a natural exterminator of the cane toad. The humble lavender beetle may hold the key to its extinction. Native to the Northern Territory, this species of beetle is poisonous to amphibians. Frogs ignore it, but the insatiable toads do not, and it kills them when eaten. Introducing the lavender beetle to areas affected by the cane toad is considered by many to be the preferred alternative, as opposed to using genetically modified viruses to exterminate the pests.

Name _____

Follow the steps below to learn how to determine the main idea and why it is important.

- There are often many ideas in text, but only one idea is the link that joins the other ideas together—this is the main idea.
- Read the text, and then ask yourself, "What is it mainly about?"
- The title is a useful clue to identifying the main idea because a good title often tells the reader what the text is about.
- Always check all possible answers before making a decision.

1. What is the main idea of this passage?

   (a) why cane toads were brought to Australia

   (b) the life cycle of cane toads in Australia

   (c) how to get rid of the cane toad

   (d) the introduction of cane toads to Australia and the devastation they have caused on the environment

2. Choose the best answer. Think about each choice carefully.

   (a) The first paragraph talks about why cane toads were introduced to Australia, but that isn't what the whole text is about. This is not a good answer.

   (b) The life cycle of the cane toad is not discussed in the text. This would not be a good answer.

   (c) The text does talk about eradicating the cane toad in the final paragraph, but this isn't what the entire text is about. This would not be the best answer.

   (d) The text talks in depth about the introduction of the cane toad to Australia and the effect the cane toad has had on many animal species. This is the best answer.

1. The main idea of paragraph 3 is:

   (a) the various native animals found in Australian bushland.

   (b) that cane toads couldn't actually do the job they were introduced to do and became pests themselves.

   (c) the devastating impact the cane toad's appetite has had on the Australian environment.

   (d) the deadly effect of the cane toad's poison on wildlife.

2. Choose the best answer. Think about each choice carefully.

   (a) The paragraph does mention some Australian native animals, but the paragraph is expressing a different idea. This is not the best answer.

   (b) This is talked about in the third sentence, not the third paragraph. This is not the right answer.

   (c) The paragraph talks about the devastation of Australia's wildlife and environment in great detail. This would be a good choice, but you need to consider all answers.

   (d) Poison is mentioned in this paragraph, but the second paragraph talks about it in depth, not paragraph 3. This would not be the best answer.

Identifying the Main Idea

Name _____

Use the strategies you learned to practice identifying the main idea. Use the clues in the "Think!" boxes to help you.

1. What is the main idea of paragraph 1?
   (a) when cane toads were first introduced to Australia
   (b) the reason the cane toad was introduced to Australia, when this happened, and the result
   (c) why the cane toad has become a pest in Australia
   (d) what was happening in Australia in 1935

> **Think!**
> What is the single idea that links the other sentences together?

2. What is the main idea of the last paragraph?
   (a) what frogs don't like to eat
   (b) the natural habitat of the lavender beetle
   (c) genetically modified viruses being used to exterminate pests
   (d) how a native insect could be used to control the cane toad population and how it works

> **Think!**
> The first sentence will be helpful.

3. Use the text and your ideas to answer these questions.
   (a) What is the title of the text?

   _____

   (b) A good title often tells the main idea. Do you think this is a good title?   ◯ Yes ◯ No
   (c) Explain why you think this.

   _____

   _____

   _____

   _____

   (d) Suggest another title that would be suitable.

   _____

> **Think!**
> The title is important. What does the title say about the passage?

4. Paragraph 4 is mainly about:
   (a) how the cane toad reproduces.
   (b) where the cane toad lives.
   (c) the increase in cane toads living in Australia.
   (d) how many cane toads live in Australia.

> **Think!**
> Which answer tells what it is mainly about and links all the ideas?

Identifying the Main Idea

Name _____

Use the strategies you have been practicing to help you identify the main idea.

1. Paragraph 2 is mainly about:
   (a) the deadly effect of the cane toad's poison on other animals.
   (b) the life stages of the cane toad.
   (c) the types of animals that can be killed by the cane toad's poison.
   (d) which animals fall victim to cane toad poison.

2. What is the main idea of paragraph 5?
   (a) what the cane toad's eggs look like
   (b) how to reduce cane toad numbers
   (c) cane toads have now spread to Kakadu National Park
   (d) the difficulties of stopping the spread of the cane toad

3. State the main idea of paragraph 6.

   _____

   _____

   _____

4. Identify the paragraphs in which the main idea is contained in the first sentence.

   Paragraph 1 ☐   Paragraph 2 ☐   Paragraph 3 ☐

   Paragraph 4 ☐   Paragraph 5 ☐   Paragraph 6 ☐

5. Think about the main idea of each paragraph. Write the number of the paragraph where you think each of these statements would best fit.

   (a) "I didn't realize how rapidly the cane toad has spread."   Paragraph ☐

   (b) "Instead of getting rid of the cane beetle, the cane toad became an even greater pest than the cane beetle ever was."   Paragraph ☐

   (c) "The cane toad has an enormous appetite."   Paragraph ☐

   (d) "Hopefully, the lavender beetle will solve the problem of the cane toad."   Paragraph ☐

   (e) "The cane toad is extremely poisonous."   Paragraph ☐

Identifying the Main Idea

Name _____

Activity: Read the passage below and complete page 30.

Robin Hood—Fact or Fiction?

1.   For many years, the tale of Robin Hood and his band of merry men have delighted children and adults all over the world. For most people, the stories are enough to bring pleasure and capture their imagination. But there are those who wish to bury themselves in research to determine the truth about the man in green. Did he really exist, or is he just the principal character of a popular legend?

2.   A number of documents, dating from the 12th to the 14th centuries, provide information that suggests such a man did exist. A 16th-century poem titled "A Gest of Robyn Hode" states that Edward II was on the throne at the time of Robin Hood's escapades in Sherwood Forest and that the king had a servant named Robyn Hood who left his service after one year. Could there be a connection? It is also recorded that supporters of the Earl of Lancaster, who was defeated by Edward II in a battle in Nottingham, fled to a forest and lived there as outlaws. Could Robin Hood have been one of these supporters?

3.   It has been suggested that the name *Robin Hood* came from a group that believed in witchcraft and wore hoods, and the name *Robin* was that of one of the gods they worshipped. Another possibility is that forest bandits used the name *Robin*, as it was a general term for "thief," and the name *Hood*, which may have been derived from "of the wood."

4.   At the time of Robin Hood's supposed existence, most of the population was illiterate, and there was very little communication between towns. The traveling bard was often the only source of information about the rest of the country. With his education and oral tradition, the bard passed on news and told stories and poems about people and things that were of interest from other areas of the country.

5.   It is possible that if the antics of Robin Hood and his band of merry men were real, they may have been retold by bards, but with each retelling, parts would have been added or taken away. With such alterations, it would not take long for any facts to be distorted so that if Robin Hood really did exist, the truth about him would be so well buried that it would take much research to unveil it. There is certainly no recorded evidence of an outlaw stealing from the rich and giving to the poor. Yet for us, this is Robin's most famous act.

6.   But does it really matter? Why is the legend of Robin Hood so popular? Is it because he may have been a true historical figure? Or is it just because it's a really good story?

Name _____

Use the strategies you learned and practiced in *Cane Toads in Australia* to help you find the main idea.

> ## Remember:
> - The main idea links all the other ideas together and tells what the text is about.
> - Read the text, and ask yourself, "What is the text mainly about?"
> - Look at the title, too.
> - Read all possible answers carefully before making a decision.

1. What is the main idea of paragraph 4?
   (a) People from different towns didn't talk to one another.
   (b) Newspapers had not yet been invented.
   (c) Most people were illiterate.
   (d) The bard was an important source of information.

> **Think!**
> What is the single idea that links the other sentences together?

2. Paragraphs 2 and 5 indicate that there may be truth in the suggestion that Robin Hood did exist. Describe the main idea of each paragraph.

   Paragraph 2: _____

   _____

   Paragraph 5: _____

   _____

3. What is the main idea of the passage?
   (a) Robin Hood did not steal from the rich and give to the poor.
   (b) Robin Hood did exist, but different bards told different versions of his adventures.
   (c) No solid evidence proves either way that the legendary Robin Hood existed or did not exist.
   (d) Robin Hood was involved in witchcraft.

4. (a) What is the title? _____

   (b) A good title often tells the main idea. Do you think this is a good title? ◯ Yes ◯ No

   (c) Explain why you think this.

   _____

   (d) Suggest another suitable title.

   _____

Name _____

Activity: Read the passage below, and use pages 32–34 to show how well you can understand words, find information, and identify main ideas.

Hadrosaurus foulkii

1.   Haddonfield is a small town in New Jersey, located on the Delaware River southeast from Philadelphia. In 1838, a man by the name of John Estaugh Hopkins was digging in a marlpit (mud rich in lime) in Haddonfield and discovered some very large bones. He displayed them in his home, not fully understanding what he had found.

2.   During the summer of 1858, a visitor to the area learned of the discovery. William Parker Foulke was that visitor, a fossil hobbyist who was very interested in the discovery 20 years prior. He went about obtaining permission from the owner of the land and gathered a team to dig up the remaining bones of the creature. The discovery became the first nearly complete dinosaur skeleton ever found (of its time).

3.   The animal that was found was larger than an elephant, with lizard- and bird-like structural features. The complete skull was never found, but based on the jaw remains, it was deemed that this dinosaur belonged to the family of dinosaurs known as the "duckbills." Paleontologist Joseph Leidy constructed the dinosaur from its remains and named it *Hadrosaurus foulkii*. The discovery of this dinosaur was important to the evolution of our knowledge of dinosaurs. Because of its almost complete skeleton, scientists, for the first time, considered the possibility that dinosaurs could be bipedal and that not all dinosaurs were quadrupedal (walking on all four legs).

4.   *Hadrosaurus* (meaning "big or sturdy lizard") lived around 80 million years ago in the late Cretaceous period. This period is known for the quick evolution of many of the well-known dinosaurs—it was also the final period to host dinosaurs. Some scientists believe that the climate dramatically changed during this period and caused the dinosaurs' (except for the crocodile) extinction.

5.   *Hadrosaurus* most likely lived in marshes and shrublands, grazing on leaves and branches. The teeth found during the dig suggest that the herbivorous dinosaur didn't simply pluck the leaves from the tree; it actually chewed its food. It was believed that the dinosaur used its front limbs for foraging and its enormous tail to help it balance (a bit like a kangaroo). Its strong hind legs enabled the *Hadrosaurus* to run quickly in order to escape predators—most likely *Tyrannosaurus rex*!

6.   The size of *Hadrosaurus* is estimated between 20 and 30 feet from nose to tail, with a height of approximately 15 feet, and a weight of around 6,000 pounds. Even though this dinosaur was so large, it is believed to have been quite placid. It traveled in a herd and may have been a good swimmer.

7.   *Hadrosaurus* probably laid eggs in a nest—much like birds of today. It is also believed that the mother protected the eggs until they hatched and then nurtured the young brood until they were ready to become independent.

8.   It has been suggested that this dinosaur was the partial inspiration for the character Jar Jar Binks in the *Star Wars* movies *The Phantom Menace*, *Attack of the Clones*, and *Revenge of the Sith*.

Name _____

> **Remember:**
> - Find and underline the word or phrase in the text.
> - Read that sentence, and some of those around it, to help you determine the meaning.
> - Substitute each of the choices in the sentence to see which one sounds correct.
> - Always check all possible answers before making a decision.

1. What does the word **bipedal** mean? (paragraph 3)
   - (a) walking on two feet
   - (b) walking on all four legs
   - (c) pedaling to get around
   - (d) unable to balance without a strong tail

2. Explain what **evolution of our knowledge** means. (paragraph 3)

   _____

   _____

   _____

3. What does the word **placid** mean in paragraph 6?
   - (a) calm and quiet
   - (b) noisy
   - (c) vicious
   - (d) light

4. Choose the best meaning for the word **host** in paragraph 4.
   - (a) entertain
   - (b) moderate
   - (c) sustain
   - (d) look after

5. Draw a picture to show the meaning of **grazing on leaves and branches** in paragraph 5.

6. Write other word(s) that could be used instead of . . .
   - (a) **deemed** in paragraph 3.

     _____

   - (b) **nurtured** in paragraph 7.

     _____

   - (c) **foraging** in paragraph 5.

     _____

Name _____

> **Remember:**
> - Underline keywords in the question to make sure that you know what information you need.
> - Find the keywords in the text, and read the information around them carefully.
> - Always check all possible answers before making a decision.

1. Who was responsible for excavating the entire skeleton?
- (a) Jar Jar Binks
- (b) Joseph Leidy
- (c) William Parker Foulke
- (d) John Estaugh Hopkins

2. Explain how *Hadrosaurus foulkii* was similar to birds of today.

_____

_____

3. What information did the teeth of *Hadrosaurus* suggest to scientists?
- (a) The teeth showed it was a carnivore.
- (b) The dinosaur actually chewed its food.
- (c) The dinosaur belonged to the duckbills.
- (d) The dinosaur plucked food from trees.

4. The Cretaceous period is famous for:
- (a) the quick evolution of many of the well-known dinosaurs.
- (b) *Tyrannosaurus rex*.
- (c) the death of the crocodile.
- (d) *Hadrosaurus*.

5. Find words in the text to complete the sentences.

(a) John Estaugh Hopkins found some very large bones while digging in a

_____ in the town of _____.

(b) The paleontologist who constructed and named the dinosaur was

_____.

(c) *Hadrosaurus* was a large dinosaur, about _____ feet tall and

weighing about _____ pounds.

(d) You would most likely have found *Hadrosaurus* living in _____ and

_____.

(e) *Hadrosaurus* belonged to the _____ family of dinosaurs.

Name _____

> **Remember:**
> - The main idea links all the other ideas together and tells what the text is mainly about.
> - The title is an excellent clue to the main idea of the text.
> - Always check all possible answers before making a decision.

1. Paragraph 6 is mainly about:
    (a)   the size of *Hadrosaurus foulkii.*
    (b)   how *Hadrosaurus foulkii* was a good swimmer.
    (c)   the size and behaviors of *Hadrosaurus foulkii.*
    (d)   the behaviors of *Hadrosaurus foulkii.*

2. What is the main idea of the last paragraph?
    (a)   *Hadrosaurus foulkii* was the star of a popular movie.
    (b)   Writers of the *Star Wars* movies used *Hadrosaurus foulkii* as partial inspiration when designing the character Jar Jar Binks.
    (c)   Writers of the *Star Wars* movies helped to uncover *Hadrosaurus foulkii* for their movies.
    (d)   *Hadrosaurus foulkii* was used in lots of *Star Wars* movies.

3. What is paragraph 1 mainly about?

    _____

    _____

4. State the main idea of paragraph 4.

    _____

    _____

5. Use the text and your ideas to answer these.

    (a)   What is the title of the text? _____

    (b)   A good title often tells the main idea.

        Do you think this is a good title?   ◯ Yes   ◯ No

    (c)   Explain why you think this. _____

    _____

    (d)   Suggest another title that would be suitable. _____

Sequencing

Lesson Objective

- Students will sequence events.

Background Information

This section demonstrates how to determine the order in which events occur, sometimes using time markers and other strategies to identify the relationship between events.

Knowing the sequence of events is an important and often critical factor in a reader's understanding of a text.

First, students need to determine from the question which events they are required to sequence. Then, they should locate them in the text and look for any time-marker words that could be helpful. Examples could include: *before, then, when, while, after, finally, at last,* or *following.*

Students may also find creating timelines of sections of the text or specific events a useful strategy.

Activity Answers

An Exciting Day .... **Pages 39–42**

- Practice Page: Page 41
    1. (c)
    2. (a)
    3. Last mouthful is eaten; the doorbell rings; the hairdresser arrives.
    4. They are told not to fiddle; they feel like princesses; they wave to neighbors who are watching.
    5. Auntie Jean and Gran arrive, carrying bags and boxes and hugging everybody they can reach.

- On Your Own: Page 42
    1. (4) The girls set the table.
       (2) The girls take showers.
       (3) The girls collect the cutlery and place mats from the kitchen.
       (1) The girls jump out of bed.
    2. (b)
    3. (c)
    4. She collects dresses from bedroom; she removes dresses from the plastic bags; the girls get dressed; the bridesmaids help Sally into her dress.

Make a Rocket Boat .... **Pages 43–44**

- Try It Out: Page 44
    1. (c)
    2. Fill the tube three-quarters full with hot water; replace the cork tightly.
    3. (b)
    4. Loop tape and use it to attach both candles to the boat.
    5. Ask an adult to light the candles.

Assessment Answers

Sequencing .... **Page 58**
    1. (c)
    2. Handed Bob 10 dollars for scratchers; took them to the counter and scratched them; put two in the trash and tore up the third.
    3. (3) Ricky fell off his bike laughing. (4) Ricky rode home at lightning speed.
       (2) Ricky frantically shook Bob's hand. (1) Ricky watched the green flashing zeros.
    4. (d)

Lesson Objective

- Students will compare and contrast people, places, and events.

Background Information

The ability to compare and contrast the information provided in a text enhances the reader's understanding of that text and is an important comprehension skill students need to practice.

Students are required to categorize information in order to determine what some people, places, and events have in common or how they differ.

Graphic organizers are a very useful tool for identifying similarities and differences, particularly Venn diagrams, T-charts, and compare-and-contrast charts.

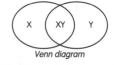

Venn diagram

same	different

T-chart

A	B	A	B
compare		contrast	

Compare-and-Contrast chart

Activity Answers

The Platypus and the Echidna..**Pages 45–48**

- Practice Page: Page 47
  1. (d)   2. (c)
  3. The platypus is in the common area as it dwells in land and water. The echidna is only in the land section.
  4. Possible answers: Echidnas have long snouts; platypuses have bills; echidnas are covered in coarse hair and spines; platypuses are covered in fur; platypuses have tails; platypuses have webbed feet.
  5. They both are very sensitive and help the animals to find food.

- On Your Own: Page 48
  1. (c)
  2. (a) The echidnas use their front claws for digging, and the platypus uses its front feet for propelling itself through water.
     (b) The echidnas use their back claws for grooming, and the platypus uses its back feet for steering and braking (when in the water).
  3. (c)

	Platypus	Echidna
Eats insects		X
Uses feet as brakes	X	
Suckles milk	X	X
Young are puggles		X

  4. A male platypus releases venom from spurs on the inside of each hind leg, and an echidna rolls into a ball, showing its spikes.
  5. They lay eggs that hatch after 10 days' incubation. Both babies suckle milk from the mother.

Movie Reviews...**Pages 49–50**

- Try It Out: Page 50
  1. (d)   2. (b)
  3. Possible answers: European city, cobbled streets, churches, a bridge, picturesque scenery
  4. Both men are fathers who are heroic and trying to save their families.
  5. (a) A villain has an agenda that is affecting a family.
     (b) One is about an international villain who wishes to assassinate a leader; the other is about a leader of a company who wishes to demolish a shop and build apartments.

Assessment Answers

Finding Similarities and Differences...**Page 59**
  1. (c)   2. (c)
  3. She has more time to spend with her children and is laughing more.
  4. Similar—living at home with his family, mother still nagging him;
     Different—has a car and an iPod®, is attending college now, probably has quit job at Foodco (since it was torture!)

Predicting

Lesson Objective

• Students will use information from a text to predict outcomes not explicitly stated in the text.

Background Information

To be able to predict outcomes, often in terms of the probable actions or reactions of specific characters, students need to focus on content and understand what they read. They need to monitor their understanding as they read, constantly confirming, rejecting, or adjusting their predictions.

The focus of this section is on teaching students how to locate and use the information provided in the text to determine probable outcomes and then to evaluate their predictions.

Students need to be able to locate specific information related to an issue and/or characters, using keywords and concepts. Their predictions should not be wild guesses, but well-thought-out, relevant ideas based on the information provided and some prior knowledge.

If students' answers differ, it is suggested that they check again to see why their answer varies from the one given. If they can justify their answer, teachers may decide to accept it.

Activity Answers

Penguin Island ....**Pages 51–54**

• Practice Page: Page 53
  1. (d)
  2. (d)
  3. She is most likely still looking at the eggs or trying to read her penguin book.
  4. (d)
  5. Answers will vary. Possible answer: No, because they are embarrassed and they will get into trouble.

• On Your Own: Page 54
  1. (b)
  2. (d)
  3. (c)
  4. Answers will vary. Possible answer: Mrs. Flea may blow her whistle again and try to find out when Jess was last seen and then walk the whole class back to the caves and look for Jess.
  5. Answers will vary. Possible answer: When Mrs. Flea realized students were missing, her stomach flipped in terror, so it is unlikely that she would like to take students back to Penguin Island for a night walk.

A Vacation to Remember ....**Pages 55–56**

• Try It Out: Page 56
  1. (d)
  2. (b)
  3. Answers will vary. Possible answer: No; as he is having too much fun on the farm and has a roost to build.
  4. Answers may vary. Possible answer: Most likely, he will want to go back.
  5. Possible answers: accident when on back of "ute;" accident on a motorbike; pinched by yabby claw; kangaroo hits the "ute;" bitten by spider from old planks of wood, etc.

Assessment Answers

Predicting ....**Page 60**
  1. (d)
  2. (c)
  3. Happier, laughing more, and spends more time with mother and less time alone.
  4. Answers will vary. Possible answers: Now he has a car and goes to college, he probably feels happier about his situation (and less embarrassed).
  5. Answers will vary. Possible answers: He may buy Bob a new bike rack for the store to replace the rusty one or give him money.

Helpful Hints

SEQUENCING

- Make sure you know which events you need to sequence. Then find those events in the text.

- Pay attention to how they are related. Making a mental picture of what is happening in the text sometimes helps you imagine the sequence.

- Always check all possible answers before deciding on your answer.

FINDING SIMILARITIES AND DIFFERENCES

- Make sure you understand the question before you begin. Then find the keywords.

- Use a chart, table, Venn diagram, or other type of organizer, if you need to. This will help you find similarities and differences.

- Always check all possible answers before deciding on your answer.

PREDICTING

- You need to find the information that connects to the question.

- The answer will not be found in the text, but there is information you can use and think about as you read. The writer will suggest, rather than tell, what is likely to happen. You must use the details in the text to help you predict.

- Always check all possible answers before deciding on your answer.

Name _____

To fully understand what you read, you must be able to determine the order in which events occur. This is called *sequencing*.

Activity: Read the story below and complete pages 40–42.

An Exciting Day

1. Dakota and Sophie are woken up by their mother. Although it's early, the house is already full of noise. The girls jump out of bed, remembering that today is, finally, the big day!

2. After their showers, the sisters collect the cutlery and place mats from the kitchen and set the table for the special wedding breakfast their mother has organized.

3. The doorbell rings and Sally, their cousin and the bride, arrives with her wet hair in a messy bun and an exuberant grin. She hands each of the girls a small box, which they quickly open to discover a silver necklace with pink, glistening jewels.

4. Car doors slam, and the other bridesmaids bustle in through the doorway, declaring how hungry they are. Moments later, Auntie Jean and Gran arrive, carrying bags and boxes and hugging everybody they can reach.

5. Sophie and Dakota help their mother carry trays of colorful sliced fruit, baskets of warm, sweet muffins, and pancakes with all the accompaniments to the table.

6. Just as the last mouthful is eaten, the doorbell rings, and the hairdresser arrives, followed soon after by the makeup artist. The dining table is cleared, and cases of makeup, brushes, hair straighteners, curlers, and a large mirror are set up.

7. Sophie winces as her hair is pulled and pinned, while Dakota pouts her lips as pink gloss is applied. The girls' mother glides from room to room, filling glasses and chatting to all the women in her house.

8. As the hairdresser adds the final pin to Sally's hair, the doorbell rings, and the house fills with pink and white flowers. Auntie Jean announces that it's time to get dressed and collects the dresses from the bedroom. She carefully removes each one from its plastic bag. Sophie's and Dakota's dresses are white with pink ribbons around the waist and pink tulle underneath. The girls dress quickly, and they then help Sally into her magnificent white wedding gown.

9. The doorbell rings again, and the photographer has arrived. The girls are handed their bouquets and are then ushered outside to join the wedding party in the garden. The photographer barely takes a breath, talking and snapping and persuading the girls to pose this way and that.

10. Half an hour passes, and Dakota places her bouquet on the grass, declaring it's too heavy to hold. Fortunately for her, the girls' grandpa enters the garden through the side gate. He taps his watch and announces that the cars have arrived and that they are blocking the street. It's time to go!

11. The girls are bundled in the car and ordered not to fiddle with their hair, dresses, or flowers on the way to the church. Feeling like princesses, Sophie and Dakota wave to the neighbors who are standing on their lawns, watching the wedding parade go by.

Sequencing

Name _____

Follow the steps below to learn how to determine the sequence of events.

- Remember that the order in which things happen is very important.
- Make sure you understand which events you need to sequence.
- Look in the text to find the events listed as possible answers and underline them.
- You will need to determine how these events are related. There may be some time-marker words, such as *then*, *before*, or *next*, in the text to help you.
- Always check all possible answers before making a decision.

1. Which event happens **after** Sally, the bride, arrives at the house?

   (a)   The girls take showers.

   (b)   The girls set the table.

   (c)   Their mother wakes them up.

   (d)   The girls open their presents.

2. Choose the best answer. Think about each choice carefully.

   (a)   The girls take showers before Sally arrives at the house, so this cannot be the right answer.

   (b)   The girls set the table before Sally arrives at the house, so this cannot be the right answer.

   (c)   Their mother wakes them up before they take showers and before Sally arrives. This is not the right answer.

   (d)   Sally gives the girls their presents after she arrives, so they open them after that. This is the best answer.

1. What happens **just before** the girls are given their bouquets?

   (a)   Sally is helped into her wedding dress.

   (b)   Auntie Jean says it is time to get dressed.

   (c)   The photographer arrives.

   (d)   The girls go out into the garden.

2. Choose the best answer. Think about each choice carefully.

   (a)   Sally is helped into her dress some time before the girls are handed their bouquets. Did it happen just before? Check all answers before deciding.

   (b)   The girls get dressed before they are given their bouquets, but did it happen just before?

   (c)   The photographer arrives after the doorbell rings and just before the girls are handed their bouquets. This is probably the right answer.

   (d)   The girls take their bouquets out into the garden with them, so this is not the right answer.

Name _____

Use the strategies you learned to practice sequencing. Use the clues in the "Think!" boxes to help you.

1. What happens **first**?
   (a) The house fills with flowers.
   (b) The photographer arrives.
   (c) Sally's hair is pinned.
   (d) The girls put their dresses on.

> **Think!**
> Underline each event in the text to determine which one happens **first**.

2. Which one of these events happens **between** Sophie wincing as her hair is pulled and pinned and her mother filling glasses?
   (a) Dakota pouts her lips as pink gloss is applied.
   (b) The house fills with flowers.
   (c) The hairdresser arrives.
   (d) The girls get dressed.

> **Think!**
> Find the part of the text that describes Sophie wincing and her mother filling glasses. Read what happens between these two events.

3. Which three things happen **just before** the makeup artist enters the house?

   • _____

   • _____

   • _____

> **Think!**
> Find the event in the text, and read the text immediately before it.

4. Explain what happens **after** the girls are bundled into the car.

   _____

   _____

   _____

   _____

> **Think!**
> You will need to read the last paragraph to answer this question.

5. What happens **just after** the other hungry bridesmaids arrive?

   _____

   _____

> **Think!**
> Find the event in the text, and read the text immediately after it.

Name _____

Use the strategies you have been practicing to help you determine the sequence of events.

1. Use the numbers 1 to 4 to show the order in which these events happen in the text.

   ☐ The girls set the table.

   ☐ The girls take showers.

   ☐ The girls collect the cutlery and place mats from the kitchen.

   ☐ The girls jump out of bed.

2. Which event takes place last?
   (a) The dining table is cleared.
   (b) Brushes and makeup are placed on the table.
   (c) The makeup artist arrives.
   (d) The hairdresser arrives.

3. Which event should be listed as event number 2 in the box below?
   (a) The girls are bundled in the car.
   (b) The photographer directs the girls to pose this way and that.
   (c) The girls' grandpa enters the garden through the side gate.
   (d) Sally is helped into her magnificent white gown.

   > Event 1. Dakota places her bouquet on the grass.
   >
   > Event 2. _____
   >
   > Event 3. The girls' grandpa taps his watch.
   >
   > Event 4. The girls' grandpa says that the cars are blocking the street.

4. List the four things that happen right after Auntie Jean announces it's time to get dressed.

   • _____

   • _____

   • _____

   • _____

Sequencing

Name _____

Activity: Read the instructions below and complete page 44.

Make a Rocket Boat

Follow these directions to make a steam-powered "rocket boat." You will need adult assistance for several steps.

Materials needed:

- metal tube (with one open end)
- 2 pieces of stiff wire, 2 feet long
- plywood
- cork
- 2 tea candles in metal cups
- hammer
- 3 nails
- pliers
- saw
- matches
- pencil
- tape
- hot water

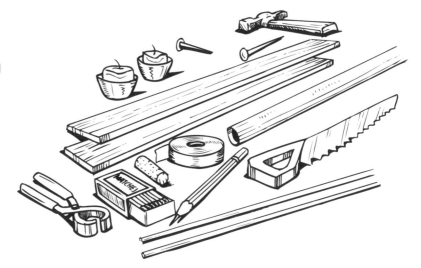

Steps:

1. Push the cork into the open end of the metal tube. Check that the cork fits very tightly in the tube. Poke a hole all the way through the cork using a nail. Ask an adult to help you.

2. Wrap a length of wire around one end of the metal tube about 1 ½ inches from the end. Twist the wire tightly with the pliers so it doesn't slide. Repeat with the other wire at the other end of the tube.

3. Using a pencil, sketch a boat shape onto the plywood with one square end and one triangle-shaped end for the bow of the boat. The boat should be slightly longer than the metal tube. Ask an adult to help you cut out the boat shape using the saw.

4. Carefully hammer two nails into each end of the boat. The nails will act like rudders and will help to stabilize the rocket boat.

5. Loop tape so it is double-sided, and use it to attach both candles to the boat so that they are 2 inches from either end of the boat.

6. Mount the tube above the candles by wrapping the wire around and under the boat. Use the pliers to twist the ends underneath the boat neatly. Check that the tube is directly above both candles. (When the candles are lit, they will heat the water in the tube.)

7. Remove the cork from the metal tube and carefully fill the tube with hot water so that it is three-quarters full. Replace the cork tightly. Check that the water can drip out of the hole in the cork by tipping it slightly. (Be careful! The water is hot!)

8. Using a swimming pool or filled bathtub, place the boat in the water, and ask an adult to light the candles with matches.

9. Wait a little while, and then watch the rocket boat go!

Name _____

Use the strategies you learned and practiced in *An Exciting Day* to help you determine the sequence of events.

> **Remember:**
> * Make sure you understand which events you need to sequence.
> * Find the events in the text and underline them.
> * Determine how the events are related. Look for time-marker words.
> * Check all the possible answers before making a decision.

1. Which of these things should you do right after you have used the pliers to twist the wire underneath the boat?

   (a) Mount the tube above the candles.

   (b) Wrap the wire under and around the boat.

   (c) Check to make sure the tube is directly above the candles.

   (d) Remove the cork from the tube.

> **Think!**
> Find the part of the text where the pliers are used to twist the wire underneath the boat and read on.

2. Write the missing steps between the ones listed below. Make sure they are in sequential order.

   * Remove the cork from the metal tube.

   * _____

   * _____

   * Check that the water can drip out the hole in the cork.

3. What is the first thing you should do after you have collected the materials needed for the rocket boat?

   (a) Poke a hole through the cork using the nail.

   (b) Push the cork into the open end of the metal tube.

   (c) Ask an adult to help you.

   (d) Check the cork fits tightly in the tube.

4. Explain what you should do between hammering the nails into the boat and mounting the tube above the candles.

   _____

   _____

   _____

5. What should be done directly after the boat is placed in the water?

   _____

Name _____

To help you understand what you read in a text, you sometimes need to think about how things are alike or how they are different and make comparisons.

Activity: Read the passages below and complete pages 46–48.

The Platypus and the Echidna

1.   A mammal is an animal that has a backbone (vertebrate) and, when young, suckles milk from its mother. The platypus and the echidna are both Australian mammals. Read on to find out more about these interesting creatures.

Platypus

2.   The platypus divides its time between water and land. It uses webbed front feet to propel itself through water and its back feet to steer and to act as brakes. The webbing cleverly folds back, so the platypus is able to walk (or waddle) on land.

3.   The platypus is covered in fur and has a rubbery bill (resembling a duck's beak) with extra-sensitive nerves in it to help the animal feel its way around and find food. The platypus feeds by using its claws to dig in streams and river beds. Although it has a toothless jaw, it eats small shrimp, insect larvae, and freshwater crawfish.

4.   When a male platypus becomes an adult, it uses spurs on the inside of each hind leg to defend itself from predators. Venom from the spur is released when the platypus feels threatened.

5.   The platypus is a special type of mammal—a monotreme. A monotreme is unlike other mammals, as it does not give birth to live young. Instead, the female lays soft-shelled eggs (usually two at a time). After 10 days, the platypus hatches. It is held close to the mother by her large tail and suckles on milk from her abdomen. The offspring leave the safety of the burrow when they are about 17 weeks old.

6.   Many Australians may have never seen a platypus in the wild, but they probably touch one every day—on their 20-cent coin!

Echidna

7.   An echidna is covered with coarse hair and spines. It has a long snout that acts as a mouth, nose, and it can even be used to pound down large prey to a smaller size for eating. The snout is very sensitive and can feel vibrations, which helps the echidna discover the ant hills and logs where it feeds. Its long, sticky tongue flicks in and out of narrow holes to collect ants and termites.

8.   With short limbs and large, sharp claws, the echidna is a powerful digger. The front claws are used for digging and the rear ones for grooming.

9.   An echidna is a monotreme (a special type of mammal). The female lays one soft-shelled egg that is deposited straight into her pouch. 10 days later, the young echidna, called a *puggle*, hatches and suckles milk from the mother. The echidna is moved from the pouch to its own burrow. Spines appear at about 50 days old. The mother continuously returns to feed the puggle until it is seven months old and can leave the burrow.

10.   The echidna's spines help to protect it from predators. The spines are most effective when the echidna rolls into a ball, which it does when it feels threatened.

11.   Echidnas are usually found in Australilian bushland and are sometimes spotted by people when the creature tries to cross a country road. You can see an echidna on the Australian 5-cent coin!

Finding Similarities and Differences

Name _____

Follow the steps below to learn how you can organize information in order to make it easier to answer questions about similarities and differences.

- Make sure you understand the question and underline the keywords.
- Sometimes, it is easy to see how things are different or the same if you are comparing two things. However, if there are three or more things to compare, it can be helpful to organize the information in a chart. Two examples are shown below.
- Always check all possible answers before making a decision.

1. Which two things do an echidna and a platypus have in common?

(a) They live only on land and lay eggs.

(b) They eat shrimp and live on land.

(c) They are monotremes and eat shrimp.

(d) They are monotremes and lay eggs.

	Platypus	Echidna
Lives only on land		
Eats shrimp		
Monotreme		
Lays eggs		

2. Choose the best answer. You will find it useful to put marks on the chart above to show information from the text.

(a) Both animals lay eggs, but only the echidna lives only on land. This is not the correct answer.

(b) Only the platypus eats shrimp and the echidna lives only on land. This cannot be the correct answer.

(c) Both animals are monotremes, but only the platypus eats shrimp. This cannot be the correct answer.

(d) Both animals are monotremes and lay eggs. This is the correct answer.

---

1. Use the information in the Venn diagram to help you find the answer.
Which is true *only* for the platypus?

(a) has a large tail and has a pouch

(b) lays eggs and digs with claws

(c) covered in fur and has a large tail

(d) covered in fur and is a monotreme

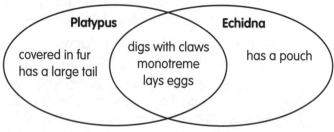

2. Choose the best answer.

(a) The platypus has a large tail, but it's the echidna that has a pouch. This is not the right answer.

(b) They both lay eggs and both dig with their claws. The question is asking what is true *only* for the platypus. This is not the right answer.

(c) The platypus has a large tail and is covered in fur, and the echidna does not have either feature. This is the correct answer, but be sure to check all answers before deciding.

(d) The platypus is covered in fur, but both the platypus and the echidna are monotremes. This is not the right answer.

46

Finding Similarities and Differences

Name _____

Use the strategies you learned to practice finding similarities and differences. Use the clues in the "Think!" boxes to help you.

1. Echidnas and platypuses have this in common:
    - (a) They both eat freshwater crawfish.
    - (b) They both use their back claws for grooming.
    - (c) They are both covered in coarse hair.
    - (d) They both are featured on an Australian coin.

    > **Think!**
    > See which piece of information is in the text for both animals.

2. Which two things are only true for echidnas?
    - (a) They are mammals and usually lay two eggs.
    - (b) They have powerful claws and a rubbery bill.
    - (c) They lay one egg and are monotremes.
    - (d) They are monotremes and have webbed feet.

    > **Think!**
    > Read only the text about echidnas to find the answer for this question.

3. Complete the Venn diagram and then explain what it means.

    Echidna and Platypus Habitats

    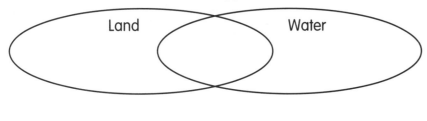

    Land   Water

    > **Think!**
    > Find the parts of the text that say where each animal lives, and write *echidna* and *platypus* in the correct space.

    _____

    _____

4. Describe three ways that the appearance of a platypus and echidna are different.

    - • _____

    - • _____

    - • _____

    > **Think!**
    > Find the parts of the text that describe the way each animal looks.

5. Explain the similarities between a platypus's bill and an echidna's snout.

    _____

    _____

    _____

    > **Think!**
    > Find the parts of the text about the snout and the bill, and see what is similar about them.

Name _____

Use the strategies you have been practicing to help you identify similarities and differences.

1. The echidna and the platypus are similar because:
    (a) they both find food in streams and river beds.
    (b) they are both covered in coarse hair.
    (c) they both lay soft-shelled eggs.
    (d) they both use their tails to keep their offspring close.

2. Describe the differences in how the following are used . . .

    (a) Platypus's front feet vs. echidna's front claws: _____

    _____

    (b) Platypus's back feet vs. echidna's rear claws: _____

    _____

3. Complete the chart to help you complete the sentence.
    Platypuses and echidnas are similar because:

	Platypus	Echidna
Eats insects		
Uses feet as brakes		
Suckles milk		
Young are puggles		

    (a) they both eat insects.
    (b) they both use their back feet as brakes.
    (c) they both suckle milk from the mother.
    (d) both their young are called *puggles*.

4. What is different about the way an echidna and a platypus react when threatened by a predator?

    _____

    _____

    _____

5. What are some similarities regarding how echidnas and platypuses produce and raise their offspring?

    _____

    _____

    _____

Name _____

Activity: Read the movie reviews below and complete page 50.

Movie Reviews

The Snake and the Fox

1. In the new action thriller *The Snake and the Fox*, Judd Browning is compelling as Dr. Bradley Fox—dentist and family man by day and Special Agent Fox by night.

2. Choosing the magical European city of Prague as the backdrop for this fast-paced film was pure genius by director Bo Bentley. The chase across the Charles Bridge to medieval Prague, with its cobbled streets and mystical churches, is "edge of your seat" explosive!

3. The evil perpetrator, "The Snake" (a.k.a. veteran actor Stirling PJ Smith), masters the villainous role as he attempts to terminate the peacekeeping leader of the United Nations, Mia Kifo. To do so, he must destroy anyone in his path, which includes, of course, Agent Fox. So dastardly is the Snake that he also sets his sights on Fox's family—wife Abigail (the English beauty, Nicola Carrington) and their twin daughters. Fox is the ultimate action hero who must rescue his family and protect Mia so that she can continue her work in bringing peace to all nations.

4. With fantastic scenery and superb casting, every scene in this 107-minute masterpiece is captivating. It's a holiday blockbuster!

5. *The Snake and the Fox* opens on December 12 in cinemas across the country.

Saving Gelato

1. Set in Europe in the striking city of Florence, the likeable Marcello family live a simple life. They work hard running their successful gelato (ice cream) shop amid the cobbled streets and historical churches of Florence. Marcello Gelato is as familiar to the locals of Florence as Ponte Vecchio, the magnificent bridge that crosses the river Arno.

2. The slow-moving plot of this quietly dramatic piece seems familiar—big company trying to buy smaller company to demolish it for profit, wiping out tradition and a family's livelihood.

3. Head of the Buildco Corporation, Kit Tyson (Stirling PJ Smith) is notorious as the power-hungry executive trying to replace the Marcellos' store with high-rise apartments.

4. The audience will empathize with the plight of the Marcello family, especially the father, Marco Marcello (played superbly by Adam LaPlaglia) who heroically attempts to stop Buildco's plans and save the family business.

5. Director and writer Jacinta Stockworth is a wonderful storyteller who has created a film that will captivate audiences. *Saving Gelato* is a picturesque film with believable characters—it is all heart!

6. *Saving Gelato* opens on December 2 in cinemas across the country.

Finding Similarities and Differences

Name _____

Use the strategies you learned and practiced in *The Platypus and the Echidna* to help you recognize similarities and differences.

Remember:
- Make sure you understand the question and underline keywords.
- Use a chart or Venn diagram if you need to.
- Check all possible answers before making a decision.

---

1. The villains in both movies are similar because:

   (a) they both run large companies.

   (b) they both want to assassinate someone.

   (c) they are both trying to destroy a business.

   (d) they are both played by Stirling PJ Smith.

Think!
A chart containing each of the four possibilities might be useful to answer this question.

---

2. Which two things are true for only one of the movies?
   (a) The movie is set in Florence and stars Nicola Carrington.
   (b) The movie stars Nicola Carrington and opens on December 12.
   (c) The movie opens on December 12 and is directed by Jacinta Stockworth.
   (d) The movie is set in Florence and opens on December 12.

3. List three things the settings of the two movies have in common.

   • _____

   • _____

   • _____

4. Explain the similarities between the characters Dr. Bradley Fox and Marco Marcello.

   _____

   _____

   _____

5. Explain how the plots of the two movies are . . .

   (a) similar: _____

   _____

   _____

   (b) different: _____

   _____

   _____

Predicting

Name _____

As we read, it is important to pay attention to what is happening and to think about what may happen next.

Activity: Read the story below and complete pages 52–54.

Penguin Island

1. The class trotted across the wooden bridge, staring down though the cracks at the black ocean. Ashlea and Tom walked side by side, while Jess lagged behind, trying to read a book about penguins by flashlight.

2. At the start of the night walk, Mrs. Flea, their teacher, bellowed strict instructions to the class about staying together, being safe and sensible, and not distressing the penguins. She warned them that if anyone broke the rules, parents would be called in the morning to come and take their child home from camp.

3. Tom reached out and tickled Ashlea's side, making her giggle and blush.

4. As they walked along the boundary of Penguin Island, the track started to slope upwards.

5. "There's one!" yelled Maddy, frantically pointing.

6. A sleeping seagull standing on one leg woke and flew away from the group. Everyone laughed, and poor Maddy's face turned the color of a tomato. She was glad to be in darkness.

7. The class stopped to lean against some railings, listening to the ocean crash against the rocks far below. Tom grabbed Ben's jacket and pushed his top half over the edge of the railing and then quickly pulled him back. Ben squeezed his eyes tightly shut and breathed in sharply.

8. "Tom! Don't!" Ashlea whispered sternly as loudly as she could without alerting Mrs. Flea.

9. They continued to walk along the track. Mrs. Flea pointed out the nooks and crannies in the boulders, which looked like small caves. The adventurous students ducked inside them.

10. "I've found some eggs!" yelled Ben, leaning over to grab one.

11. "Don't touch them!" ordered Jess. She crouched into the cave, shined her flashlight at the eggs, and enthusiastically reached for her book. The students took turns looking inside the cave at the eggs until Mrs. Flea moved them along.

12. As students continued to walk, the caves disappeared, and most of the class concluded that there were actually no penguins on Penguin Island. They began to mess around with their flashlights. Maddy dropped hers and heard it rolling down the slope.

13. "Why me . . . ?" she whimpered sadly to herself.

14. "Don't even think about chasing after it, Maddy. We'll lose you over the edge!" said Mrs. Flea, as she tried to do a headcount in the dark. Her stomach flipped in terror.

15. "Freeze on the spot!" she yelled into the wind. "Shine your flashlights and see who is missing!"

16. Flashlights were flying everywhere, blinding the children and exposing their frozen faces.

17. "Tom's gone!" Ben informed them, secretly smiling. "And Ashlea and Jess, too."

18. Mrs. Flea blew her whistle. Moments later, Ashlea and Tom appeared, running down the track together, looking embarrassed.

19. "Unbelievable!" Mrs. Flea growled at the two students. "Well . . . where is Jess?"

20. Ashlea and Tom looked back up the path toward the caves.

21. "She wasn't with us," mumbled Ashlea.

22. The rest of the class pointed their flashlights at the edge of the path, illuminating the cliff and the long drop to the ocean and rocks below.

Name _____

Follow the steps below to learn how to make a prediction about what may happen next.

- The answers are not in the text, so you can't just read them, but there is information for you to use and think about.
- You need to find information related to the question. (This could be underlined.)
- Think hard! What is the writer suggesting might happen?
- Always consider all possible answers before making a decision.

1. Which of these things would Mrs. Flea most likely do next?
   (a) tell the class to go on ahead and meet her at the bridge
   (b) use her phone to call Jess's parents
   (c) order Tom and Ashlea to go back up the path and find Jess
   (d) blow her whistle again

2. Choose the best answer. Think about each choice carefully.
   (a) Mrs. Flea had ordered the class to stay together, so it is unlikely she would ask them to separate. This is not a good answer.
   (b) A phone has not been mentioned in the text, and it is unlikely Mrs. Flea would call Jess's parents so quickly. This is not a good answer.
   (c) Mrs. Flea wouldn't want them to separate, and she was upset with Tom and Ashlea since they had disobeyed the rules. It is unlikely she would ask them to go looking for Jess. This is not a good answer.
   (d) Mrs. Flea had blown her whistle once before, and two children had come, so it is probable that it will work again. This is the best answer.

1. Which of these things would most likely have happened if Mrs. Flea saw Tom push Ben at the railings?
   (a) She would have laughed.
   (b) She would have ignored Tom.
   (c) She would have told Tom he had broken the rules, and she would be calling his parents when they got back to camp.
   (d) She would have told Tom to apologize to Ben and moved the class along.

2. Choose the best answer. Think about each choice carefully.
   (a) Mrs. Flea had been clear with her warnings at the start of the night walk, so it's unlikely that she would laugh at Tom's behavior. This is not the right answer.
   (b) Mrs. Flea had been clear with her warnings at the start of the night walk, so it's unlikely that she would ignore Tom's behavior. This is not the right answer.
   (c) Tom had not behaved sensibly and was being unsafe. It is most likely that Mrs. Flea would inform him that he had broken the rules and his parents would be called. This is a good answer, but you must check all of the choices.
   (d) Mrs. Flea had set punishments for certain behavior at the start of the night walk, so it seems unlikely that she would have let Tom off with just an apology. This is probably not the right answer.

Predicting

Name _____

Use the strategies you learned to help you predict what will happen. Use the clues in the "Think!" boxes to help you.

1. Which of these things would Maddy be most likely to do if she thought she saw another "penguin"?

    (a) run up to it and pick it up

    (b) point at it and alert the class to her sighting

    (c) ignore it completely

    (d) look more closely to confirm that it was a penguin

> **Think!**
> Read paragraph 6 about the seagull and see how Maddy reacted.

2. If Ben were to walk near railings again, what is he least likely to do?

    (a) walk at the back of the group

    (b) walk next to Mrs. Flea

    (c) keep away from the railings and far away from Tom

    (d) walk near Tom and as close to the railing as possible

> **Think!**
> Find the part of the text in paragraph 7 that describes how Ben reacted to being pushed.

3. Predict what you think is the most likely reason for Jess's disappearance.

    _____

    _____

    _____

> **Think!**
> Refer back to the text, and look for the parts that mention Jess.

4. Which of these things is Mrs. Flea most likely to say to Jess when she is found?

    (a) "Did you have a good time?"

    (b) "I hope you found some penguins while you were missing."

    (c) "Please apologize to the class for making them wait for you."

    (d) "You have broken the rules, Jess! Where were you?"

> **Think!**
> Read parts of the text that mention Mrs. Flea to help you answer this question.

5. Do you think Ashlea and Tom now think disappearing from the group was a good idea? Give reasons for your answer.

    _____

    _____

    _____

    _____

> **Think!**
> Read paragraphs 2 and 18.

Name _____

Use the strategies you have been practicing to help you make predictions.

1. Imagine Jess came across sleeping penguins. Which of these things would she least likely do?
   (a) alert the class of her findings
   (b) find a stick and poke them with it
   (c) look in her book to find out which breed they are
   (d) crouch down and study them

2. Which of these things is most likely to happen when Jess is found?
   (a) The class will continue their tour of the island.
   (b) Jess will tell the class about her adventures.
   (c) Mrs. Flea will order Jess, Ashlea, and Tom to walk back to camp.
   (d) Mrs. Flea will ask Jess where she was, then tell her she is being sent home tomorrow.

3. Which of these things would Maddy be most likely to do if she was given another flashlight?
   (a) mess around with it again
   (b) say she didn't want one
   (c) hold on to it carefully
   (d) shine it in her classmates' faces

4. Explain what you think Mrs. Flea will most likely do next. Give reasons for your answer.

   _____

   _____

   _____

   _____

5. What do you think Mrs. Flea would say if she were asked to take a class on a night walk of Penguin Island again? Give reasons for your answer.

   _____

   _____

   _____

   _____

Predicting

Name _____

Activity: Read the diary entries below and complete page 56.

A Vacation to Remember

Alex Stuart, age 11

Sunday, January 4

1. We arrived during the hottest part of the day, and the flies couldn't get enough of our sweaty skin! Uncle Joe's farm *looked* just how I imagined an Australian farm in the summertime to look—lots of sheds; big machinery; rusty, forgotten trucks; and dry, brown fields in every direction!

Wednesday, January 7

2. Today we drove around the farm checking sheep. It was Joe, Dad, and me, so I was allowed to sit in the back of the "ute" with Rex, the sheepdog, instead of sitting inside the vehicle. We moved a mob of sheep closer to a dam so that they could have a drink. One sheep was lagging behind. Joe bellowed instructions at Rex, who chased the sheep and pinned it down so we could check it.

Friday, January 9

3. Today was cool! I rode on the four-wheeler motorbike with Dad. Joe was on the two-wheeler with Rex on the back. We rode along the fence line and put some yabby nets out in a dam. A yabby is an Australian crawfish. While we were there, Joe gave me a string with some meat on the end, and I caught three yabbies with it! (One had the most enormous claw!)

Saturday, January 10

4. This afternoon, we collected the yabbies from the nets and scored three buckets' worth! I watched Aunty Sue and Mom cook them, and then I peeled them for our dinner. Delicious! On the drive back from the dam, six big kangaroos were bouncing alongside us! I've never been so close to a roo before. It was awesome!

Tuesday, January 13

5. The shearers came today, and they worked like machines! I helped the other volunteers pick up wool from the floor, and when Mom and Aunty Sue finally brought lunch, I felt like I could eat a horse! At the end of the day, Uncle Joe said I deserved to be paid for my hard work and gave me $50!

Friday, January 16

6. I helped Dad and Uncle Joe build a chicken coop today. We used a big machine to dig the holes, and then we cemented in the posts. (Mom stood and watched the whole time to make sure I didn't get too close to the machine and "lose a limb"!) Dad and I found an old gate that fit the coop perfectly. We pulled the chicken wire around the pen and attached it. Tomorrow, I'm going to build a roost from some old planks of wood I found behind the tractor shed.

7. I can't believe I only have three more days left on the farm *before* we fly all the way *back* home!

Name _____

Use the strategies you learned and practiced in *Penguin Island* to help you make predictions.

> **Remember:**
> - You need to find and underline the information related to each question.
> - The answer is not in the text, but there is information you can use and think about.
> - The writer will suggest, rather than tell, what is likely to happen.
> - Check all possible answers before making a decision.

1. If Alex's mom had gone with them to check sheep, predict which of these situations would have been most likely to happen.

   > **Think!**
   > Read Wednesday, January 7 to help you answer this question.

   (a) Alex and his mom would have sat in the back of the "ute" together.
   (b) Mom and Rex, the dog, would have sat in the back of the "ute" together.
   (c) Alex and his mom would have sat inside the vehicle without their seatbelts on.
   (d) Alex and his mom would have sat in the back of the "ute" along with Rex, the dog.

2. What is Alex least likely to do on Saturday, January 17?
   (a) go back to the dam to catch more yabbies
   (b) collect planks of wood from behind the tractor shed
   (c) help his mom and Aunty Sue with the cooking
   (d) ask to borrow the four-wheeler bike to look for more kangaroos

3. Now that Alex has $50, do you think he will want to leave the farm to go shopping and spend his money? Give reasons for your answers.

   _____

   _____

   _____

4. Predict and write what you think Alex will most likely say if his parents ask him if he wants to go back to the farm for their next vacation.

   _____

5. Imagine Alex had been involved in some type of accident during his vacation. Use the text to help you predict two likely things that could have gone wrong during his time on the farm.

   - _____

   - _____

Name _____

Activity: Read the story below, and use pages 58–60 to show how well you can sequence, find similarities and differences, and predict.

Luck of the Draw!

1. Ricky pulled the card from the envelope and shook it. A 10-dollar bill fell to the floor, which he pocketed as he walked toward the front door. "Must thank Grandma," he reminded himself.

2. "Where do you think you're going?" called his mother from the kitchen. "I'm late, and you've got to pick up Georgia from soccer practice, AND you've got to start work in half an hour!"

3. As if Ricky needed reminding. He had been stocking the shelves at Foodco for three weeks now, and it was torture! Employees weren't even allowed to use an iPod®—not that Ricky had one—yet!

4. Ricky grunted a response to his mother and jumped on his bike. He was 18 today, and he could finally buy scratcher lottery tickets. He had been watching his mother scratch them at the dinner table every payday for years. He would secretly cross his fingers and toes while she scratched, but his silent wishing never worked. His mother still had to work the night shift, meaning she was always tired, and his little sister was left home alone a lot. Although he had grown used to his mother being grumpy, he worried about Georgia—he hadn't heard her laugh in months.

5. As Ricky pedaled up the street, he passed a group of kids he had gone to school with. They were standing by their cars and chatting, probably about the fun they were having at college. Ricky had been accepted to go but had to defer to work full-time and help out his mom. Ricky pulled his cap lower over his eyes and kept pedaling. He'd had his license for six months now, but buying a car was an unrealistic dream.

6. At the store, he locked his bike up to the rusty rack and asked Bob, the manager, for 10 dollars' worth of "scratchers." Ricky took them straight to the counter and started scratching. First ticket went into the trash, then the second, and in frustration, he tore up the third. With slumped shoulders, Ricky walked toward the door of the shop.

7. "Hey, Ricky," Bob called. "Always check them through the machine. Just in case."

8. Ricky shrugged and took the two tickets still in one piece from the trash and handed them over. He watched the green flashing zeros on the machine and his jaw dropped. Bob whistled. Ricky had won $500,000! He grabbed Bob's hand and frantically shook it, repeating, "I owe you, I owe you!" over and over again. Ricky grabbed the ticket, jumped on his bike, fell off laughing, jumped back on again, and rode home at lightning speed. As he skidded in the driveway, he remembered Georgia was waiting for him. "She can wait!" he thought.

9. Three months later, Ricky was in the driveway of his family's new home, washing his car. Georgia and his mother were playing soccer in the yard. His mother tried to tackle the ball away from her daughter, making Georgia have a giggle fit.

10. "Good try, Mom!"

11. "Now that I have all of this time on my hands, you can give me some lessons!" laughed her mother. She placed her arm around her daughter's waist and looked over at her son.

12. "You're going to wear the paint off that thing, you know?" she called to him. "You've got an exam to study for, mister! Hop to it!"

13. Ricky chuckled to himself. One thing never changed—his mother's nagging! He pointed at the white iPod® cords coming out from his ears, pretending he hadn't heard her. He'd just take his car for a spin around the block first, and then he would study.

14. "If only I could win some good grades," Ricky thought, laughing, as he jumped into the car and started the engine.

Name _____

> ## Remember:
> - Make sure you know which events you need to sequence, and then find and underline them.
> - Determine how the events are related. Look for time-marker words.
> - Check all possible answers before making a decision.

1. What did Ricky do immediately before walking toward the front door?
   - (a) pulled the card from the envelope
   - (b) shook the card
   - (c) put the money in his pocket
   - (d) reminded himself to thank Grandma

2. In order, list three things that happened in between the two events below.
   - Ricky locked his bike up to the rack.

   - _____

   - _____

   - _____

   - Ricky walked toward the door of the shop.

3. Write the numbers 1 to 4 to place these events in order.

   [ ] Ricky fell off his bike laughing.

   [ ] Ricky rode home at lightning speed.

   [ ] Ricky frantically shook Bob's hand.

   [ ] Ricky watched the green flashing zeros.

4. What happened just after the mother tried to tackle the ball away from Georgia?
   - (a) Ricky pointed to his iPod®.
   - (b) She placed her arm around her daughter's waist.
   - (c) Ricky started the engine of his car.
   - (d) Georgia had a giggle fit.

Name _____

Remember:

- Make sure you understand the question and underline the keywords.
- Use a chart or Venn diagram if you need to.
- Check all possible answers before making a decision.

---

1. What was common in Georgia's life before and after her brother's win?

    (a)   She spent a lot of time home alone.

    (b)   She was always laughing and happy.

    (c)   She played soccer.

    (d)   She spent a lot of time with her mother.

2. Which two things are only true about Ricky before the lottery win?

    (a)   Ricky wanted an iPod® and attended college.

    (b)   Ricky attended college and stocked shelves at Foodco.

    (c)   Ricky rode a bicycle and wanted an iPod®.

    (d)   Ricky attended college and rode a bicycle.

3. Explain how Ricky's mother's life is different after the lottery win.

    _____

    _____

    _____

    _____

4. Describe the similarities and differences in Ricky's life before and after his win.

    Similar _____

    _____

    _____

    Different _____

    _____

    _____

Name _____

> ## Remember:
> - You need to find and underline the information related to each question.
> - The answer is not in the text, but there is information you can use and think about.
> - The writer will suggest, rather than tell, what is likely to happen.
> - Check all possible answers before making a decision.

1. Now that Ricky has won the money, what is he least likely to do?
   - (a) buy more lottery tickets
   - (b) drive his car to college
   - (c) sell his iPod®
   - (d) stock shelves at Foodco

2. Predict what Ricky's mother said after he told her about the win.
   - (a) "What are you wasting your money on scratchers for?"
   - (b) "Well-done, son. Now get to work! You're late!"
   - (c) "Let's go and pick up Georgia and tell her the good news!"
   - (d) "Let's go and celebrate!"

3. Predict one way life will be different for Georgia now.

   _____

   _____

4. On his drive, imagine Ricky passes in the street the friends he went to school with. How do you think he would be feeling? Give reasons for your answer.

   _____

   _____

   _____

   _____

5. Predict one way Ricky might thank Bob for telling him to put the tickets through the machine.

   _____

   _____

Drawing Conclusions

Lesson Notes

Lesson Objective

- Students will make judgments and reach conclusions based on facts and details provided in a text.

Background Information

This section demonstrates how to decide on the meaning of facts and details provided in a text and how to build up evidence in order to make judgments and reach conclusions about the information.

Students also need to be able to search for evidence to support a particular conclusion by locating the relevant information in the text and then making judgments about it.

In higher-order comprehension skills such as this, answers are not always immediately obvious, and discussion about why one answer is judged to be the best should be encouraged. However, teachers may decide to accept another answer if a student can provide the necessary evidence to support the answer he or she has given.

Activity Answers

Mona Lisa .... Pages 65–68

- Practice Page: Page 67
  1. (c)
  2. (b)
  3. The *Mona Lisa* is in a bulletproof glass casing. It is also extremely famous and very valuable, therefore high-tech security measures are most likely in place throughout the museum.
  4. (a)–(b) Answers will vary. Possible answer: Although it is showing signs of aging, it is very protected and cared for.

- On Your Own: Page 68
  1. (d)
  2. (b)
  3. (c)
  4. It is protected (bulletproof glass, etc.); six million people a year come to see it; it is also very valuable to France.
  5. (a)–(b) Answers will vary.

The Worst Day of the Year! .... Pages 69–70

- Try It Out: Page 70
  1. (c)
  2. (c)
  3. Pete was unable to jump over the bar, while children much younger than Pete could make it over.
  4. made him go to Sports Day; gave him salad for lunch; was planning on going for a walk with the dogs the next day.
  5. (a)–(b) Answers will vary.

Assessment Answers

Drawing Conclusions .... Page 84
  1. (c)
  2. (b)
  3. they rescued the people from the dam just after the fire swept through.
  4. Answers will vary. Possible answer: She was scared and distracted while driving in a big hurry.
  5. people were injured; properties were lost; and thousands of acres of land were damaged.
  6. (a)–(b) Answers will vary.

Lesson Objective

- Students will summarize text by linking important information and identifying the main points.

Background Information

To be able to summarize text successfully, students first need to be clear about what they are being asked to do and what form their answer should take. (For example, a one-word answer or a more detailed explanation may be required.) It will help if they underline the keywords in the question.

They then need to locate any relevant information in the text, underline it, and establish how it is linked. Words such as *while*, *but*, *and*, *when*, and *as* may be significant in establishing how the information is linked. Unnecessary and irrelevant information should be omitted and the main points established for inclusion in the summary.

Students may need to locate information throughout the entire text in order to summarize the main points for some questions.

Answers may vary and will require teacher review. Those given below are provided as a guide to the main points.

Activity Answers

Trapped Miners Freed After 14 Days...**Pages 71–74**

- Practice Page: Page 73
  1. (d)
  2. (c)
  3. Larry Knight's body found; new tunnel blasted; six explosives set off; Brant and Todd try to clear rocks; they write goodbye letters on their clothes
  4. (a)–(b) Answers will vary.

- On Your Own: Page 74
  1. (d)
  2. (c)
  3. (b)
  4. April 25: Rockfall at Beaconsfield mine; Todd and Brant trapped in mine
     April 27: Larry Knight's body found; rescuers set off explosives to make a tunnel
     April 30: Men are found alive by thermal imaging cameras; given fresh food and clothes
     May 9: Brant and Todd are freed from mine
     After May 9: Brant and Todd tell their story and earn lots of money in the process

David Copperfield — Master of Illusions..**Pages 75–76**

- Try It Out: Page 76
  1. (d)
  2. Walking through Great Wall of China; making Statue of Liberty disappear; levitating across the Grand Canyon; surviving a fall over Niagara Falls; escaping Alcatraz Penitentiary
  3. (c)
  4. David and two assistants were robbed. David used magic to make his wallet "disappear."
  5. Answers will vary. Possible answers: Teaching magic at a university at the age of 16; being in a musical that broke box office records; very popular television show; his spectacular illusions; his museum and Project Magic

Assessment Answers

Summarizing..**Page 85**

  1. (b)
  2. (c)
  3. 8 a.m—Radio announces evacuation; Midmorning—Firefighters from nearby cities join local fighters; 2 p.m.—Three people leave their car and jump in dam and are rescued; Nightfall—Three people in hospital, firefighters still trying to control blaze
  4. Writing report cards; hears about fire and evacuation; puts books in car; leaves in hurry; crashes into tree; unconscious; rescued by two people; recovers in hospital.
  5. Answers will vary.

Lesson Objective

- Students will make inferences about what is most likely to be true based on information provided in the text.

Background Information

Inferences are opinions about what is most likely to be true and are formed after careful evaluation of all the available information. Students need to realize that because there is no information that tells them the actual answer, their inferences may not be correct. They have to determine what makes the most sense given the information provided and to then look for details to support their decisions. They may need to use some prior knowledge to help them determine their answer.

The focus of this section is on teaching students how to use contextual information, both written and visual, to determine what they believe to be true. They then must find further evidence to support their decisions.

Student answers will need to be checked by the teacher, but some possible answers have been provided as a guide.

Activity Answers

Bindiyup Rock .... **Pages 77–80**

- Practice Page: Page 79
  1. (d)
  2. (c)
  3. Answers will vary. Possible answer: No, because she had brought a hair dryer and there were obviously no power outlets.
  4. the family who had been on their speedboat at the lake
  5. Ellie was found by the lake; she could have drowned.

- On Your Own: Page 80
  1. (d)
  2. (b)
  3. (d)
  4. Answers will vary. Possible answers: she was distracted by rocks and weeds; she is only three years old; she doesn't know how long a "few minutes" takes.
  5. Answers will vary. Possible answers: upset; exhausted; anxious; scared; sad.
  6. (a)–(b) Answers will vary.

Ignorance .... **Pages 81–82**

- Try It Out: Page 82
  1. (d)
  2. (b)
  3. (a) No
     (b) Answers will vary. Possible answer: They thought he would look like a monster with fangs and flames.
  4. (a)–(b) Answers will vary. Possible answer: Yes, because the children were ignorant of the old man in the house.
  5. (a)–(b) Answers will vary.

Assessment Answers

Making Inferences .... **Page 86**

1. (c)
2. (d)
3. Answers will vary. Possible answer: She needed books and records to write the report cards and thought she might lose them if the school burned down in the fire.
4. Answer will vary. Possible answer: Yes, as they decided to leave their car.
5. Answers will vary. Possible answer: proud; heroic; relieved, etc.
6. Answers will vary. Possible answer: weather could change; fire still out of control; putting their safety first.

DRAWING CONCLUSIONS

- Make sure you understand what it is you are drawing conclusions about.
- Look in the text to find the facts and details.
- Make decisions about what they mean.
- Always check all possible answers before deciding on your answer.

SUMMARIZING

- Check the text to be sure you understand the question. Then, find the keywords.
- Find information in the text that is most important to your understanding of it. Decide how it is connected.
- Take out any unnecessary details or unconnected information.
- Always check all possible answers before deciding on your answer.

MAKING INFERENCES

- The answers are usually not in the text, but there is information that will give you clues to think about.
- Find the answer that makes the most sense and is supported by the text.
- Always consider all possible answers before making a decision.

Drawing Conclusions

Name _____

When you draw conclusions, you are making decisions or judgments after considering all the information. We make conclusions about what we read by finding facts and details in the text, taking it all into consideration, and then making judgments about it.

Activity: Read the passage below and complete pages 66–68.

Mona Lisa

1.   Possibly the most famous painting in the world, the *Mona Lisa* is an oil painting by the artist Leonardo da Vinci. It shows a woman with a mysterious smile in front of a misty, mountainous landscape.

2.   Leonardo painted the *Mona Lisa* in Florence, Italy between 1503 and 1506. Unlike his other paintings, da Vinci did not sell it immediately but kept it with him at all times. About 10 years later, he allowed the King of France, King François I, to buy the masterpiece and display it in his castle.

3.   The *Mona Lisa* was passed down through the royal line to King Louis XIV. After the French Revolution, it was displayed at the Louvre Museum in Paris, France. In 1800, the powerful ruler of the French army and government, Napoleon Bonaparte, took it from the museum to hang in his bedroom. When he lost his power, the *Mona Lisa* was returned to the Louvre.

4.   During the Franco-Prussian War in 1870, the painting was hidden in a small town somewhere in France.

5.   The *Mona Lisa* was well known, but it was not until it was stolen from the Louvre in 1911 that it achieved fame all over the world. The painting was missing for two years (and believed destroyed) until a man tried to sell it to an art dealer in Florence. It was later discovered that the man once worked at the Louvre Museum and had hidden in a broom closet after the museum closed and walked out with the painting.

6.   Throughout history, the biggest question surrounding the painting has been (and still is) "Who was Mona Lisa?" Despite thorough research by art historians, only theories can be offered. Some historians believe "Lisa" was the wife of a wealthy silk dealer in Florence, while others think she is a self-portrait of Leonardo da Vinci or possibly his mother.

7.   In 1956, acid was thrown onto the painting, damaging the lower section. In the same year, a rock was thrown at it, altering an area near the figure's left elbow.

8.   Before the painting went on tour to the United States and Asia in 1962, it was insured for 100 million dollars, entering the Guinness World Records for the most valuable painting ever to be insured.

9.   The mysteries behind the *Mona Lisa* continue to captivate art historians and the world. In 2005, infrared cameras were able to "see through" da Vinci's finished painting, showing the different versions of "Lisa" he had painted over.

10.   *Mona Lisa*'s complexion has darkened, and the painting is losing its luster over time, but everyone who sees her is still mesmerized by her hypnotic smile—a smile that can now be seen on posters, postcards, coffee mugs, and much more. The *Mona Lisa* also finds its way into the storylines of many songs, films, and books.

11.   Today, the painting hangs in the Louvre Museum behind an air-conditioned, bulletproof glass casing. It is viewed by about six million people each year.

Name _____

Follow the steps below to learn how you can practice drawing conclusions.

- Conclusions are decisions you make after careful consideration of facts and details in the text.
- Make sure you understand what it is you are drawing conclusions about.
- Look in the text to find the facts and details and underline them.
- You will need to make decisions about what they mean.
- Always check all possible answers before making a decision.

1. You can conclude that the *Mona Lisa* became so famous because:

   (a) it is the most beautiful painting ever painted.

   (b) the artist was the famous Leonardo da Vinci.

   (c) it was stolen, and so much mystery surrounds it.

   (d) it is in songs, films, and books.

2. Choose the best answer. Think about each choice carefully.

   (a) It is a beautiful painting, and people would want to see it, but this doesn't quite explain why it became so famous. This is a possible answer, but there is probably a better one.

   (b) The artist was very famous, and all his paintings would be valuable, but this doesn't explain why this one painting became so famous.

   (c) The theft of the painting would have been widely reported, and people all around the world would have heard about it and been interested. This would have added to the mystery about the identity of the subject. This is a very good answer.

   (d) The painting had to be well known before people wanted to write films, songs, and books about it. This cannot be the right answer.

1. What would be the best reason for why the *Mona Lisa* was removed from the museum during the Franco-Prussian War and hidden in a small town in France?

   (a) so it could be cleaned

   (b) so a copy could be made of it

   (c) so it wouldn't fall into the hands of the enemy

   (d) in case there was a fire

2. Choose the best answer. Think about each choice carefully.

   (a) During a war would be a strange time to clean a very valuable piece of art, and this is not mentioned in the text. This is not a good answer.

   (b) Again, during a war would be a strange time to copy a very valuable piece of art, and it is not mentioned in the text. This is not the best answer.

   (c) The painting was so valuable to France that it would have been hidden away from enemies who may have wanted it for themselves. This is a very good answer.

   (d) This is a reasonable answer, but there could have been a fire at any time or in any place. This is not the best answer.

Drawing Conclusions

Name _____

Use the strategies you learned to practice drawing conclusions. Use the clues in the "Think!" boxes to help you.

1. You can conclude Leonardo felt strongly about the *Mona Lisa* because:

   (a)   it was of his mother.

   (b)   he spent four years painting it.

   (c)   he did not part with it for many years.

   (d)   he knew many people wanted it.

> **Think!**
> Read paragraph 2 to help you answer this question.

2. You can conclude Napoleon Bonaparte took the painting from the Louvre because:

   (a)   it was worth a fortune.

   (b)   he had so much power in France at the time that he could just take it.

   (c)   he wanted to display it for everyone to see.

   (d)   he wanted to keep it safe.

> **Think!**
> There is information to help you reach this conclusion in paragraph 3.

3. In 1911, an employee of the Louvre stole the *Mona Lisa* by hiding in a broom closet at the museum. Explain why this is less likely to happen today.

_____

_____

_____

_____

> **Think!**
> Read the text again, and underline the sections that mention how valuable the painting is.

4. The *Mona Lisa* is over 500 years old.

   (a)   Do you think the *Mona Lisa* will be viewed by tourists in another 500 years?

      ◯ Yes   ◯ No

   (b)   Explain how you reached this conclusion.

_____

_____

_____

_____

> **Think!**
> Read the last two paragraphs to help you reach your conclusion.

Name _____

Use the strategies you have been practicing to help you draw conclusions.

1. You can conclude that the employee of the Louvre who stole the *Mona Lisa* waited two years to sell it because:
   (a) he misplaced it.
   (b) he wanted time to admire its beauty.
   (c) he was already rich and didn't need the money.
   (d) he was waiting for the publicity about the theft to die down.

2. Why was the *Mona Lisa* insured for 100 million dollars?
   (a) so it could be in the Guinness World Records
   (b) because it was leaving the museum and more at risk of theft
   (c) so if it was damaged once again it could be repaired
   (d) to pay for the infrared camera inspection

3. Why is the identity of Mona Lisa in da Vinci's masterpiece still unknown?
   (a) because people are happy to just enjoy the beauty of the painting and don't really care about her identity
   (b) because art historians aren't looking hard enough to find out the truth
   (c) it was painted over 500 years ago, so it is hard to find records for that time
   (d) because people keep disagreeing on the facts

4. You can conclude that the *Mona Lisa* is very valuable to the Louvre Museum because . . .

   _____

   _____

   _____

5. (a) Would you like to go to the Louvre in Paris to see the *Mona Lisa*?

   ◯ Yes   ◯ No

   (b) Explain how you reached this conclusion. _____

   _____

   _____

   _____

Drawing Conclusions

Name _____

Activity: Read the email below and complete page 70.

The Worst Day of the Year!

From:	Pete
To:	Ben
Subject:	Sports Day!
Date:	Friday, December 2

Hey Ben,

1.   I couldn't believe it! I could have spent the day in the air-conditioned library surfing the Internet, but instead Mom made me go to Sports Day, and it was TORTURE!

2.   Miss Baker's eyebrows almost shot off her face when she saw me standing on the sports field in shorts and sneakers. She looked me up and down and told me that, as my team was the "Tree Frogs," I should be wearing a green shirt like the other kids—not a red one! How was I to know?

3.   The kids in the slime-colored shirts and I found the green tent, and right away I knew I was in trouble! Mr. Henderson (the sports teacher I've told you about before) was our leader for the whole day. I recalled all the creative excuses I've used to skip his class this year, and I hoped he didn't decide today was payback time!

4.   I managed shot put, discus, and long jump okay. I thought I saw some of the moms shaking their heads when I couldn't quite make it over the bar onto that squishy, blue mattress for high jump. (I don't know how those younger kids made it over!)

5.   At least (I thought), I had my usual sandwich and doughnut to look forward to. But, NO! Mom decided that today she would inflict even more torture on me by giving me a salad for lunch! It was warm, and there wasn't even any meat in it!

6.   After lunch the "slime group" kept walking around the field doing tunnel ball, the sack race, the put-the-stick-in-the-cone-(I don't know what it's called)-race, and then with only an hour to go, I saw it. The moms and dads were lining up their chairs along the edge of the track. My chest felt tight, and I started to sweat even more than I already was! Surely Mr. H wouldn't do that to me! I don't run! I never run! You know me—I don't even walk if I can help it!

7.   Well, he did do it to me, and I wanted to dig a hole in the field and bury myself in it! The 100 m, 200 m, 400 m, and then the 800 m. Can you believe people started to go home while I was still doing the last lap of the 800 m?

8.   As I said, Ben, it was the worst day of the year! Tomorrow is Saturday, and Mom said we are taking Scruffy and Bella to the park for a walk. I think she will need a wheelbarrow to push me around!

9.   I hope your day was better than mine!

Pete   ;-)

Name _____

Use the strategies you learned and practiced in *Mona Lisa* to help you practice drawing conclusions.

Remember:

- Make sure you understand the question and what you are drawing conclusions about.
- Look in the text for facts and details and underline them.
- Decide what they mean.
- Check all possible answers before making a decision.

1. You can conclude that Pete didn't wear a green T-shirt to Sports Day because:
   (a) he doesn't have a green shirt.
   (b) he didn't know it was Sports Day.
   (c) he'd never been to a Sports Day before, and he had no idea of the color of the team he was on.
   (d) he was trying to make Miss Baker upset with him and send him home.

   Think!
   There is information in paragraphs 2 and 3 to help you reach this conclusion.

2. What would be the best reason why Pete started to sweat when he saw the parents lined up along the edge of the track?
   (a) He started to feel sick and feverish.
   (b) He had just finished a race.
   (c) He was embarrassed about them watching him run around the track.
   (d) He was worried they would call him names from the sidelines.

3. What would be the best reason why the moms were shaking their heads at Pete during the high jump?

   _____

   _____

   _____

4. Complete the sentence by giving three reasons from the text.
   You can conclude Pete's mother is trying to make her son healthier because she . . .

   - _____

   - _____

   - _____

5. (a) Do you think Pete likes to exercise?   ◯ Yes   ◯ No
   (b) Explain how you reached this conclusion.

   _____

   _____

Summarizing

Name _____

Summarizing is stating the main ideas or facts without using many words. We need to link the important ideas and decide which are the main points.

Activity: Read the passage below and complete pages 72–74.

Trapped Miners Freed After 14 Days

1.   On April 25, 2006, a minor earthquake triggered a rockfall at the Beaconsfield Gold Mine in Tasmania, Australia. Seventeen men were working in the mine that day and 14 walked out alive. Serious concerns were held for three missing miners—Larry Knight, Todd Russell, and Brant Webb.

2.   At the time of the collapse, Todd and Brant were working a half mile underground in the metal cage of a machine known as a *teleloader*. Thousands of small rocks fell, trapping the men inside the cage. Todd's legs were covered in rocks, and Brant was knocked unconscious for a short time. When he woke, the pair systematically removed the individual rocks off of them. Thankfully, groundwater was dripping from some of the overhead rocks, so the men used their helmets to collect it.

3.   For two days, rescuers used remote-controlled earth movers to search for the three missing men, and on April 27, the body of Larry Knight was found. Many believed it would be a miracle if Todd and Brant were found alive.

4.   The rescuers decided the original tunnel was unsafe, so they blasted a new tunnel. Six large explosives were detonated, dislodging rocks surrounding the cage the two miners were in. They tried to clear the rocks as new ones fell in their place. After some time, Todd and Brant believed the explosions being detonated to rescue them would actually kill them, so they wrote goodbye letters to their families on their clothing.

5.   On April 30, five days after the rockfall at the Beaconsfield Gold Mine, Todd Russell and Brant Webb were miraculously found to be alive! The families of the two men rejoiced, and the residents of Beaconsfield celebrated in the streets. Special thermal imaging cameras that detect heat were used to find the men in the rubble. A hole was drilled into the cage, and fresh food and water, batteries for their headlamps, dry clothes and blankets, newspapers, and letters from the miner's families were passed through. The men asked for music players, the local sports results, and humorously, a newspaper to "look for another job."

6.   Although Todd and Brant could be seen and spoken to, it was believed that trying to rescue them through the new tunnel would cause another rockfall. The rescuers stopped using explosives and worked around the clock, carefully drilling—knowing the slightest mistake could cause a catastrophe. It was a slow process as they could only drill at a rate of about 15 inches per hour. Hundreds of people and journalists with their news teams waited in anticipation at the mine site, hoping to catch a glimpse of the freed miners. They waited another nine days!

7.   On May 9, rescuers, who had been painstakingly drilling upwards with hand tools, retrieved Brant Webb and Todd Russell from the cage and escorted them to the surface. Friends, family, the media, and all of Australia watched as the two men (incredibly) walked out of the mine with fists punching the air in triumph. That same day, Todd Russell attended the funeral of his colleague, Larry Knight.

8.   After they were freed, the men were offered million-dollar deals to tell their story, which they did on news shows in Australia and America. A worldwide book deal was agreed, and a film of the men's survival story followed.

Name _____

Follow the steps below to learn how you can identify the main points and summarize text.

- Make sure you understand the question and underline the keywords.
- Look for information in the text, and decide what is important and how it is connected.
- Omit any unnecessary or unconnected information.
- Always check all possible answers before making a decision.

1. Which sentence would best be left out of a summary about the rescue of the two miners?

   (a) The Beaconsfield Mine is in Tasmania, Australia.

   (b) The rock fall occurred on April 25, 2006.

   (c) Todd and Brant spent 14 nights underground before they were freed.

   (d) The residents of Beaconsfield celebrated in the streets.

2. Choose the best answer. Think about each choice carefully.

   (a) Where the rescue took place is an important fact that needs to be in the summary. This is not a good answer.

   (b) The date of the rockfall is an important fact and should be in the summary. This is not the best answer.

   (c) Readers will want to know how long the men were trapped in the mine, so this must be in the summary. This is not a good answer.

   (d) This sentence is interesting but not essential for the summary. This is the best answer.

1. How could the men's condition after they were discovered alive by the rescuers on April 30 best be summarized?

   (a) The men were thirsty and hungry.

   (b) The men were unconscious.

   (c) The men were in good spirits.

   (d) The men were very upset with the mining company.

2. Choose the best answer. Think about each choice carefully.

   (a) The text mentions that the men could drink water dripping from the rocks, so they weren't thirsty, although they would have been hungry. This is not the best answer.

   (b) Brant had been unconscious for a short time but not when they were discovered alive. This is not a good answer.

   (c) As the men requested newspapers to "look for another job" in a joking manner, they were most likely in good spirits. This is probably the best answer, but you need to check all answers.

   (d) Perhaps the men were upset with the mining company, but this is not mentioned in the text. This is not the best answer.

Summarizing

Name _____

Use the strategies you learned to practice summarizing. Use the clues in the "Think!" boxes to help you.

1. Which sentence best summarizes why the men were able to survive underground for the first five days?
   (a) They had each other for company.
   (b) They only had minor injuries.
   (c) They could see with their headlamps.
   (d) They used their helmets to collect water to drink.

> **Think!**
> Read paragraph 2 to help you choose an answer.

2. Which sentence best summarizes why the rescuers stopped using explosives and started drilling to free the miners?
   (a) Explosives were too expensive.
   (b) The explosives were too noisy.
   (c) Drilling was safer.
   (d) Drilling was quicker.

> **Think!**
> Look carefully at the information in paragraph 6 to help you decide on an answer.

3. Use short phrases to make a summary of what happened between April 27 and April 30.

   • _____
   • _____
   • _____
   • _____
   • _____

> **Think!**
> You will find the main points for your summary in paragraphs 3 and 4.

4. (a) Write a sentence that summarizes the efforts of the men who rescued the trapped miners.

   _____
   _____
   _____
   _____

   (b) Write a sentence that summarizes your opinion of the rescuers.

   _____
   _____
   _____

> **Think!**
> Think about what the rescuers had to do to get to the trapped miners.

Name _____

Use the strategies you have been practicing to help you summarize text.

1. Which sentence would best be left out of a summary explaining how the men were rescued?
    (a) The rescuers used large explosives to create a new tunnel.
    (b) Cameras that detect heat found the two men in the rubble.
    (c) Rescuers drilled at a rate of 15 inches per hour.
    (d) Hundreds of journalists waited to film the men once they reached the surface.

2. Which sentence best summarizes why Todd and Brant wrote goodbye letters to their families on their clothes?
    (a) They missed their families.
    (b) They had no paper to write on.
    (c) They believed they may never see their families again.
    (d) They wanted to tell their families about the accident.

3. Which two words best summarize the people who rescued Brant and Todd from the mine?
    (a) friendly and determined
    (b) determined and brave
    (c) cautious and stubborn
    (d) stubborn and friendly

4. Summarize the events that took place on each of these dates.

    April 25: _____

    _____

    April 27: _____

    _____

    April 30: _____

    _____

    May 9: _____

    _____

    After May 9: _____

    _____

Summarizing

Name _____

Activity: Read the passage below and complete page 76.

David Copperfield—Master of Illusions

1.   David Copperfield was born David Seth Kotkin on September 16, 1956, in New Jersey.

2.   From a young age, David had a passion for magic and entertaining. He was performing magic to audiences in his hometown when he was 12, and by 16, he was teaching magic at New York University.

3.   Two years later, David won the lead role in a Chicago-based musical, *The Magic Man*, which broke box office records. He continued to work, tirelessly touring, performing his magic and illusions to audiences across America. This led to his own television show. *The Magic of David Copperfield* became an extremely popular and regular television special across the globe. David performed his greatest magical illusions, such as walking through the Great Wall of China, making the Statue of Liberty disappear, and levitating across the Grand Canyon. He also survived a plunge over Niagara Falls and was the first person to escape Alcatraz Penitentiary.

4.   David claims that he does not use any camera tricks or visual effects and that each illusion takes about two and a half years to perfect. His incredible "flying" illusion was the result of seven years' work.

5.   The world has recognized David Copperfield's amazing talent with many awards, a star on the Hollywood Walk of Fame, and a lifelike wax figure of himself at Madame Tussaud's in London.

6.   David created the International Museum and Library of the Conjuring Arts, which houses many of the world's collections of historical documentation and artifacts about magic. He also founded Project Magic, which is run in over 1,000 hospitals around the world. The project helps to rehabilitate people, assisting them regain the use of their hands and improve their hand-eye coordination by teaching them magic tricks to practice.

7.   In April 2006 in Florida, David and two of his assistants were robbed at gunpoint. The assistants gave the gunmen their money and other valuables, but in a police statement, David explained how he used his famous "sleight-of-hand" trick to make his wallet disappear. The men were identified and later arrested.

8.   David continues to do approximately 500 performances each year, and he has been named as one of the world's highest paid celebrities, with earnings of approximately $57 million a year. David Copperfield combines storytelling, spectacular illusions, and entertaining theater to be one of the world's greatest illusionists.

Name _____

Use the strategies you learned and practiced in *Trapped Miners Freed After 14 Days* to help you summarize information.

> ## Remember:
> - Make sure you understand the question and underline the keywords.
> - Look for information in the text, and decide what is important and how it is connected.
> - Omit any unnecessary or unconnected information.
> - Always check all possible answers before making a decision.

1. Which sentence would best be left out of a summary of how David Copperfield became the "Master of Illusions"?
   (a) David had a passion for magic and entertaining at a young age.
   (b) David taught magic at New York University.
   (c) David became well known by performing his magic shows across the country.
   (d) David has his own star on the Hollywood Walk of Fame.

2. Make a summary list of David Copperfield's most spectacular illusions.

   - _____
   - _____
   - _____
   - _____

3. Which sentence best summarizes how David creates his illusions?
   (a) He finds the ideas for the illusions in his antique books about magic.
   (b) He bases his illusions around famous landmarks.
   (c) He spends a lot of time perfecting the illusions without using camera tricks.
   (d) He tries to think of illusions that are extremely dangerous.

4. Write a short summary of the events that occurred in April 2006.

   _____

   _____

5. Write a paragraph that summarizes David Copperfield's greatest achievements.

   _____

   _____

   _____

   _____

   _____

> ## Think!
> Underline David's achievements in the text. Choose the ones that are the most important, and write your summary.

Making Inferences

Name _____

When we read, we often make decisions about what we think is most likely to be true based on the information given in the text. This is called *making inferences.*

Activity: Read the story below and complete pages 78–80.

Bindiyup Rock

1. Reece was awakened by a car door slamming right outside his window. He was up, dressed, and out front in record time. Dad was loading the back of the car with the camping gear. Reece looked around and picked up the sleeping bags and put them in the car, making his dad stop what he was doing and stare at him.

2. It was the start of the long weekend, and Reece, his little sister Ellie, and his parents were going camping up to Bindiyup Rock along with his cousin, aunt, and uncle.

3. The trip was long, and there was nothing much to look at. Ellie chatted the whole way in her special three-year-old language, sang bits of nursery rhymes, and put a sticky, wet jelly bean in Reece's hair.

4. After some time, Reece noticed how thick the bushes on either side of them were becoming. They passed a lake and saw people for the first time in over an hour. There was a speedboat pulling two kids along in a rubber ring. Dad kept on driving until they came to a clearing. Reece saw it first—a big rock that looked quite like a paler, smaller version of a huge rock they saw on their last camping trip. Reece spotted his cousin, Josh, and as soon as the car stopped, he jumped out and ran towards him.

5. Mom got out and surveyed the dusty, bare ground of the campsite. She laughed. "Are you sure this is it?" she asked her husband, who nodded. "Well, … I should have left my hair dryer at home then!"

6. While the adults were setting up the tents and lighting the barbeque, Reece and Josh were itching to explore the area around them. Every time they disappeared, one of their moms would yell at them to come back and do something. In the end, the moms gave in. Reece's mom told the boys to take Ellie for a walk around the base of the rock while they prepared dinner.

7. The boys whooped with excitement, and they each grabbed one of Ellie's hands and headed towards the rock. They surveyed it as they walked but had to stop every few minutes so Ellie could show them some "interesting" stone or weed she had discovered. Eventually, Reece found a spot in the rock they could climb up. The boys told Ellie to wait exactly where she was and that they would only be a few minutes.

8. About 15 minutes later, the boys jumped down from a small ledge on the rock, laughing and shouting. Josh did a big "Tarzan" roar, making Reece laugh even harder. All of a sudden, Reece's smile disappeared. He turned pale, and his stomach flipped. Ellie was gone! The boys yelled out her name over and over and decided to backtrack to the campsite.

9. When they arrived back, there were other people at the campgrounds. Reece pushed past them looking for his mom and found Ellie sitting on her lap with red eyes and a frown.

10. "She'd made it all the way to the lake, Reece," Dad said in a quiet but serious tone Reece had never heard before. "We are so lucky they found her in time."

11. Just as Reece noticed the new people were wearing life jackets, Ellie started whimpering that she wanted to go home.

12. "Let's go and find a hotel!" Mom declared.

Learning Page

Name _____

Follow the steps below to learn how to determine what is most likely to be true.

> - The answers are usually not in the text, but there is information given that will give you clues to think about. (This could be underlined.)
> - Find the answer that makes the most sense and is supported by text details.
> - Always consider all possible answers before making a decision.

1. What would be the best reason why Dad stopped and stared at Reece as he was putting the sleeping bags in the back of the car?

   (a) He was mad that Reece was helping when he should have been in bed.

   (b) He was mad that Reece was helping without asking him first.

   (c) He was surprised that Reece was out of bed.

   (d) He was surprised that Reece was helping him without being asked.

2. Choose the best answer. Think about each choice carefully.

   (a) As Reece was helping Dad, it is unlikely that he would be mad. Also, if Dad was packing the car, it was probably time for Reece to be out of bed anyway. This is not the best answer.

   (b) Once again, as Reece was helping Dad, it is unlikely he would be mad at him. This is not the best answer.

   (c) He may have been surprised that Reece was out of bed. This could be the answer, but check all the answers.

   (d) Reece was helping by putting the sleeping bags in the car when Dad stopped and stared, so he was probably surprised that his son did this without being asked. This is the best answer.

1. How was Reece most likely feeling during the trip to Bindiyup Rock?

   (a) carsick

   (b) bored and happy

   (c) bored and annoyed

   (d) annoyed and tired

2. Choose the best answer. Think about each choice carefully.

   (a) Nowhere in the text does it suggest that Reece was carsick. This is not the best answer.

   (b) He was bored as there was not much to see, but the text does not suggest he was happy. This is not the right answer.

   (c) He was bored as there wasn't much to see, and he was probably annoyed as Ellie had put a jelly bean in his hair. This is probably the best answer, but check all answers.

   (d) He was annoyed, but the text does not suggest he was tired at all. This is not the best answer.

Making Inferences

Name _____

Use the strategies you learned to help you decide what you think is most likely to be true based on information from the text. Use the clues in the "Think!" boxes to help you.

1. How was Reece most likely feeling when he realized Ellie had disappeared?

    (a) mad

    (b) annoyed

    (c) confused

    (d) worried

    > **Think!**
    > Read paragraph 8 to see how Reece reacted.

2. Most likely, why did the two moms stop the boys from exploring the new area?

    (a) They didn't want them to have any fun.

    (b) They wanted them to help the adults unpack.

    (c) They thought the boys might get lost in the wilderness.

    (d) There were worried they would be bitten by a snake.

    > **Think!**
    > Read paragraphs 4 and 6 and think about where they were.

3. (a) Do you think Dad had described the camping grounds to his wife before they left?

    ◯ Yes   ◯ No

    (b) Explain why you think this.

    _____

    _____

    > **Think!**
    > Read paragraph 5 to find out how Mom reacted when they arrived.

4. Most likely, who were the people that found Ellie by the lake?

    _____

    _____

    > **Think!**
    > Read the text again and look for details about the lake.

5. Why did Dad speak so seriously to Reece about the people finding Ellie near the lake?

    _____

    _____

    _____

    > **Think!**
    > Think about where Ellie was found.

Name _____

Use the strategies you have practiced to help you make inferences.

1. Why did Reece's mom most likely laugh when she got out of the car?

   (a)   She was happy they arrived safely.

   (b)   She was happy to be out of the car.

   (c)   The big rock looked funny to her.

   (d)   The campground was not at all what she had expected.

2. How were the boys probably feeling as they jumped down from the rock?

   (a)   exhausted

   (b)   triumphant

   (c)   scared

   (d)   hungry

3. When the boys arrived back at the campsite, why did Reece go directly to his mom?

   (a)   He had missed her.

   (b)   He was upset and wanted a hug.

   (c)   He wanted her to be the first person he told Ellie was missing.

   (d)   He was hoping Ellie had made her way back to her mom.

4. Give some reasons why you think Ellie didn't wait for the boys to return.

   • _____

   • _____

   • _____

5. Write three words to describe how you think Ellie was feeling when she was sitting on her mom's lap.

   • _____

   • _____

   • _____

6. (a)   Do you think the family will be going camping for their vacation next year? ◯ Yes ◯ No

   (b)   Explain why you think this.

   _____

   _____

Making Inferences

Name _____

Activity: Read the poem below and complete page 82.

Ignorance

---

1. Every morning they'd hurry across the road.

   As they passed by his run-down old place,

   They hoped and they prayed it would not be the day

   That they'd have to look at his face.

2. One day they caught a glimpse of him—

   Frail old man, clothes too big for his frame.

   They froze in their tracks;

   There was no turning back.

   Would the world ever be the same?

3. What scary thing was he saying?

   Where were his fangs and the flames?

   They looked at his face, which was friendly and kind,

   And he asked them to tell him their names.

4. The children looked at each other.

   They laughed as they realized the truth.

   They'd been scared by a silly old rumor,

   And now they had absolute proof!

HA HA HA!

Use the strategies you learned and practiced in *Bindiyup Rock* to help you make inferences.

> **Remember:**
> - The answers are usually not in the text, but there is information to give you clues to think about. (This could be underlined.)
> - Find the answer that makes the most sense and is supported by text details.
> - Always consider all possible answers before making a decision.

1. Why did the children hurry past the old man's house?
   - (a) because they were running late for school
   - (b) because there was a nasty smell coming from the yard
   - (c) because they thought the house was haunted
   - (d) because they were afraid of the old man who lived there

2. The children "froze in their tracks" because:
   - (a) the weather turned chilly.
   - (b) they were very frightened.
   - (c) the old man used his powers to freeze them on the spot.
   - (d) the old man was a ghost.

3. (a) When the children saw the old man, did he look the way they had imagined?
   ◯ Yes   ◯ No
   (b) Explain why you think this and give details from the text to support your ideas.

   _____

   _____

4. The title of the poem is "Ignorance," which means "lack of knowledge" and "being unaware."

   (a) Do you think the title fits the poem?   ◯ Yes   ◯ No
   (b) Explain why you think this.

   _____

   _____

   _____

   > **Think!**
   > Read the poem again and think about what the message of the poem is.

5. (a) Do you think the old man knew of the rumors about him?   ◯ Yes   ◯ No
   (b) Explain why you think this.

   _____

   _____

Name _____

Activity: Read the newspaper article below, and use pages 84–86 to show how well you can draw conclusions, summarize, and make inferences.

Devastating Fire Races Across Port Hope

A devastating fire that broke out yesterday morning continues to burn along the coast south of Port Hope.

Fire rages out of control at Port Hope

Strong, gusty winds, with speeds of 40 miles per hour, combined with scorching temperatures, created prime fire conditions. Wind-fanned flames leaped to the tops of eucalyptus trees and pines, igniting them. By 8 a.m., radio announcers had announced evacuation orders to the residents of Port Hope. By midmorning, firefighters from nearby cities had joined local fighters, working tirelessly to slow down the horrendous blaze. Their efforts were futile in such extreme weather conditions.

Local schoolteacher Grace Taylor had been in her classroom writing report cards when she heard the evacuation announcement. She filled the back seat of her car with schoolbooks and records, and then fled the school in great haste. She lost consciousness after driving into a nearby tree. Luckily, two people spotted the vehicle and revived Grace and transported her to safety.

At 2 p.m., three local residents were driving on Simpson Highway, which was officially closed at 11 a.m., and unexpectedly, came face to face with the towering wall of flame. Their life-or-death decision to abandon their car (which in many situations results in tragedy) saved their lives. The trio, two men and a woman, ran towards a dam and jumped in to escape the blaze. The three survived and were rescued by local fire authorities only minutes after the fire swept through.

By nightfall, Grace Taylor and two firefighters suffering with breathing difficulties and one with minor burns, were in Port Hope Hospital. Thousands of acres of land and several properties had been destroyed. Firefighters battled the hungry flames throughout the night but were unable to control them.

Although fire authorities are confident the blaze will be contained this morning due to an easing of the weather conditions, families continue to flee from homes in its path. ■

Name _____

> ## Remember:
> - Make sure you understand what it is you are drawing conclusions about.
> - Look in the text to find the facts and details and underline them.
> - Make decisions about what they mean.
> - Always check all possible answers before making a decision.

1. You can conclude that this fire was bigger than usual for the town of Port Hope because:
   (a) the flames were 60 feet tall.
   (b) it was talked about on the radio.
   (c) firefighters were recruited from other towns.
   (d) the Simpson Highway was closed.

2. You can conclude that the three people driving on Simpson Highway:
   (a) were lost.
   (b) didn't know the road had been closed.
   (c) knew the road was closed but wanted to see the fire up close.
   (d) wanted to drive right through the fire.

3. You can conclude the local fire authorities were very close to the fire at 2 p.m. because . . .

   _____

   _____

   _____

4. Why do you think the schoolteacher accidentally crashed into a tree?

   _____

   _____

5. You can conclude that this fire will be remembered for some time to come because . . .

   - _____

   - _____

   - _____

6. (a) Would you like to become a firefighter when you are older?   ◯ Yes   ◯ No
   (b) Explain why you reached this conclusion.

   _____

   _____

Name _____

> **Remember:**
> - Make sure you understand the question and underline keywords.
> - Look for information in the text, decide what is important, and how it is connected.
> - Omit any unnecessary or unconnected information.
> - Always check all the possible answers before making a decision.

1. Which factors best summarize the cause of the fire?
   - (a) mild temperatures and a breezy day
   - (b) very high temperatures and strong winds
   - (c) a breezy day and tall trees
   - (d) old trees and very high temperatures

2. Which sentence would best be left out of a summary of the newspaper article?
   - (a) The fire is still racing across Port Hope.
   - (b) Wind speeds of 40 miles per hour were recorded.
   - (c) Grace Taylor was writing report cards.
   - (d) Three people are in the hospital, and several properties were destroyed.

3. Use short phrases to make a summary of what happened at the following times.

   - 8 a.m.—_____

   - Midmorning—_____

   - 2 p.m.—_____

   - Nightfall—_____

4. Write a summary of what happened to Grace Taylor on the day of the fire.

   _____

   _____

   _____

5. Write a sentence that summarizes your opinion of the men and women fighting the fire.

   _____

   _____

   _____

Name _____

> **Remember:**
> - The answers are usually not in the text, but there is information that will give you clues to think about. (This could be underlined.)
> - Find the answer that makes the most sense and is supported by text details.
> - Always consider all possible answers before making a decision.

1. Why did the firefighters think their efforts were futile?
   - (a) It was too hot to work.
   - (b) There weren't enough firefighters.
   - (c) Strong winds and scorching temperatures made their task impossible.
   - (d) There were too many trees.

2. Most likely, how were the three people in the car feeling as they jumped into the dam?
   - (a) completely safe
   - (b) wet and exhausted
   - (c) excited and happy
   - (d) relieved but still frightened

3. What would be the best reason why the schoolteacher took the time to put the books and records in her car before she fled?

   _____

   _____

   _____

4. (a) Do you think the three people could see the dam from their car?   ◯ Yes   ◯ No

   (b) Explain why you think this.

   _____

   _____

5. Write a sentence describing how you think the two people felt as they were transporting Grace to the hospital.

   _____

   _____

   _____

6. Give reasons why you think families continued to evacuate their homes even though fire authorities were confident the blaze would soon be controlled.

   - _____

   - _____

   - _____

Lesson Objective

- Students will determine cause and effect and understand how they are connected.

Background Information

Students need to understand that a cause leads to an effect and that they are connected.

This section demonstrates strategies for students to use in order to find information in a text, which in turn helps them to make the connection and determine cause and effect.

They need to find and underline the keywords in questions, and then search for information in the text that makes connections between the keywords and either the cause or the effect. They need to understand that they will be given either a cause or an effect in the question, but they will need to search for the other.

Activity Answers

Global Warming ....**Pages 91–94**

- Practice Page: Page 93
  1. (d)
  2. (b)
  3. reduce greenhouse gases and global warming
  4. Some suggest it is because of human activity, and others say it is a natural occurrence.
  5. Earth will be a wonderful place for generations to come.

- On Your Own: Page 94
  1. (d)
  2. (b)
  3. Answers should list any reasons as stated in the text.
  4. Greenhouse gases would be reduced, thus reducing the effects of global warming.
  5. (c)

Letter to the Principal ....**Pages 95–96**

- Try It Out: Page 96
  1. (c)
  2. (b)
  3. Improved soil quality and healthier plants
  4. (a) They want to reduce the amount of waste caused by the children and teachers in their school.
     (b)–(c) Answers will vary.

Assessment Answers

Cause and Effect .... **Page 110**

  1. (c)
  2. (b)
  3. They contribute to the balance of the water cycle through a process called transpiration.
  4. A rainforest provides many different types of habitats, which offers opportunities for a variety of species to survive.
  5. It improves accessibility to remote areas.
  6. They can't compete for food and a home with unfamiliar species.

Lesson Objective

- Students will demonstrate their ability to identify facts and opinions and their understanding of how they differ.

Background Information

A fact is something that is true. It can be verified by referring to other information. In other words, it can be checked and be proven to be correct.

An opinion is something that someone believes to be true but cannot be verified. In other words, it is something that someone *thinks* rather than knows is true.

Students must be able to distinguish between facts and opinions in order to become critical readers. They have to engage and interact with text and read with a questioning attitude. They can then look for relationships and critically judge and evaluate what they read by identifying facts and opinions.

Critical readers become more discriminating consumers of the news media and advertising—an important life skill.

Activity Answers

Letter to the Editor ....**Pages 97–100**

- Practice Page: Page 99
  1. (a)
  2. Fact: Not all of us make it to adulthood or Not all spiders make it to adulthood.
     Opinion: It's a perilous life for a spider or A spider lives a perilous life.
  3. (a) Fact
     (b) The information can be checked using factual resources.
  4. (d)

- On Your Own: Page 100
  1. (b)
  2. (d)
  3. (a) Opinion
     (b) Answers will vary. Possible answer: It can't be proven that Miss Muffet is a scaredy cat.
  4. Fact: You'll have fewer insects inside your home.
     Opinion: Surely that would make you happy!
  5. (c)

Fight for BMX Track Continues ....**Pages 101–102**

- Try It Out: Page 102
  1. (c)
  2. Fact: I am Josh's dad.
     Opinion: I am so proud of him.
  3. (b)
  4. (a)–(b) Answers will vary.
  5. (a) Fact
     (b) The newspaper article states this. It is a fact as it can be checked in the city records.

Assessment Answers

Fact or Opinion ....**Page 111**

  1. (d)
  2. (b)
  3. (b)
  4. Fact; Answers will vary.
  5. Fact: The plants are responsible for producing 40 percent of Earth's oxygen and stabilizing the climate on the planet.
     Opinion: The plants that have evolved and adapted to the rainforest environment are amazing.

Point of View and Purpose

Lesson Objective

- Students will understand and identify the writer's point of view and purpose.

Background Information

The writer's point of view is his or her opinion about a subject. A reader should, after careful and detailed analysis of what has been written, understand and be able to identify the point of view expressed in the text.

The writer's purpose for writing explains why the text was written. It may be to express a particular point of view, to amuse, entertain, inform, persuade, instruct, describe, record information, or to explain something.

Students should be encouraged to try to determine how and what the writer was thinking and use this to help them make decisions about the writer's point of view. They should then look for details in the text to support or reject the choices they have made. (These can be underlined.)

All possible choices should be considered before a final decision is made.

Activity Answers

Too Much TV! .... Pages 103–106

- Practice Page: Page 105
  1. (a) They spend time together face to face, and they exercise together.
     (b) Their friendship is better than before.
  2. (c)
  3. for her to spend time with her grandpa and get to know him
  4. Answers will vary.

- On Your Own: Page 106
  1. (b)
  2. (d)
  3. (a)–(b) Answers will vary.
  4. (a) She feels life is more interesting and that she doesn't really need TV.
     (b) Answers will vary.
  5. (b)

Apology Letter .... Pages 107–108

- Try It Out: Page 108
  1. Answers will vary.
  2. (b)
  3. (b)
  4. Answers will vary.
  5. Answers will vary.

Assessment Answers

Point of View and Purpose .... Page 112
  1. (c)
  2. (c)
  3. (b)
  4. Answers will vary for (a) and (b).
  5. Answers will vary for (a) and (b).

Helpful Hints

CAUSE AND EFFECT

- A cause (what happened first) leads to an effect (what happened as a result of the cause). They are connected.

- You are given either a cause or an effect, and you will need to find the other.

- Look for keywords in the question. Then, find the words in the text that are connected to the keywords.

- Check all possible answers before making a decision.

FACT OR OPINION

- A fact is something that can be checked and proven to be correct.

- An opinion is what someone believes to be true, but it can't be proven. Read the text to decide what can be proven (fact) by the text.

- Always check all possible answers before deciding on your answer.

POINT OF VIEW AND PURPOSE

- Writers do not always tell you what they believe. You may have to come to this conclusion based on the information you have read.

- Look for details and information in the text to help you decide why the author may have written the text or what the author's point of view is.

- Always check all possible answers before deciding on your answer.

Cause and Effect

Name _____

Cause and effect is a phrase we use when one thing (a cause) makes something else happen (an effect). If you want to understand what you read, you must be able to determine the cause(s) and the effect(s) that happen in the text.

Activity: Read the passage below and complete pages 92–94.

Global Warming

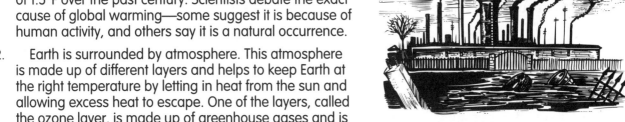

1. Global warming is a serious issue that affects every single person on the planet. It may not sound like much, but Earth's surface temperature has increased by an average of 1.5°F over the past century. Scientists debate the exact cause of global warming—some suggest it is because of human activity, and others say it is a natural occurrence.

2. Earth is surrounded by atmosphere. This atmosphere is made up of different layers and helps to keep Earth at the right temperature by letting in heat from the sun and allowing excess heat to escape. One of the layers, called the ozone layer, is made up of greenhouse gases and is like a blanket for Earth, keeping the atmosphere at a comfortable 60°F. However, when humans make extra greenhouse gases by burning fossil fuels (coal and gas), cutting down forests and rainforests, and increasing the amount of methane produced, the "blanket" becomes too thick and keeps too much of the heat in Earth's atmosphere. The job of the ozone layer is to protect Earth from harmful UVB (middle wave ultraviolet light) rays from the sun. Once damaged, this layer can no longer do its job, and the harmful rays also contribute to the heating up of Earth.

3. It has been estimated that by the year 2100, the surface temperature of Earth could be around 2°F to 11°F warmer than it is today. This warming could in fact be responsible for an increase in sea levels as the water becomes warmer and expands and glaciers and sea ice melt. This would mean that coastal cities would more than likely find themselves in deep water! Some animals and plants could become extinct due to warmer temperatures, loss of habitat, and scarce availability of food. Cooler environments could become warmer and deserts even warmer. Lakes and rivers would dry up due to the higher temperatures and rates of evaporation. There may be less rainfall, causing more droughts, making crops difficult to grow, and leading to a shortage of food. Less rainfall also means less water for drinking and bathing. It is also predicted that severe storms could become more frequent as temperatures rise.

4. The United Nations (UN) is a worldwide association of governments working together to make sure everyone in the world is kept safe and treated with respect. Part of keeping everyone safe is also making sure global warming doesn't get out of hand. In 1997, the UN met in Kyoto, Japan, to talk about global warming. The Kyoto Agreement was devised to try to ensure the amount of gases produced by industry is reduced. The agreement came into force in February 2005. It is believed that we can reduce the amount of greenhouse gases by changing the way we produce power.

5. Scientists are looking into "greenpower" energy sources. Such sources would reduce the amount of greenhouse gases being pumped out into the atmosphere. Greenpower alternatives include wave power—but scientists worry this could cause too much noise in the environment and harm the animals and wind power—but some people complain the large wind turbines are an eyesore. Other alternatives include water and solar power as well as using the gas produced from rotting trash.

6. We can help with simple measures incorporated into our everyday living. We can recycle and reuse, use vegetable scraps in a compost heap, use less water, reduce electricity use, carpool or ride a bike, and buy products that have minimal packaging. Every little bit that we can do adds up and helps our environment.

7. By finding a solution to global warming, we can make Earth a wonderful place for many generations to come!

Name _____

Follow the steps below to learn how you can identify cause and effect.

- A cause leads to an effect, and they are connected.
- You will be told one, and you will need to identify the other.
- Look for keywords in the question and underline them.
- Find words in the text that are connected to the keywords.
- Always check all possible answers before making a decision.

1. What causes lakes and rivers to dry up? (paragraph 3)

    (a) too much snow and rainfall

    (b) too many animals drinking the water

    (c) severe storms suck up all the water

    (d) higher temperatures and evaporation rates

2. Choose the best answer. Think about each choice carefully.

    (a) Snow and rainfall would actually help to fill the lakes and rivers, so this would not be the right answer.

    (b) Could you imagine how many animals would have to drink from a lake or river to cause it to become empty? Way too many, so this would not be a good answer.

    (c) Yes, the text said there would be severe storms, but these would more than likely cause water to be added to lakes and rivers. This is not the best answer.

    (d) The text talks about higher temperatures and rates of evaporation working to dry up rivers and lakes. This would be the best answer.

1. What is the effect of damaging the ozone layer?

    (a) Our blankets make us too hot at night.

    (b) UVB rays contribute to the heating of Earth.

    (c) Greenhouse gases increase.

    (d) Fossil fuels would cause more damage.

2. Choose the best answer. Think about each choice carefully.

    (a) The blankets on our beds would have no effect on the environment, so this would not be the right answer.

    (b) The text says if the ozone layer is damaged, the effect is that it cannot protect Earth from UVB rays, which contribute to its heating. This is a good answer, but be sure to check all answers.

    (c) The increase in greenhouse gases causes the problem with the ozone layer, not the other way around. This is not the right answer.

    (d) Burning fossil fuels causes greenhouse gases to increase. This doesn't explain the effect of damaging the ozone layer. This is not the right answer.

Cause and Effect

Name _____

Use the strategies you learned to practice identifying cause and effect. Use the clues in the "Think!" boxes to help you.

1. What is a possible effect of using wave power?
   - (a) Surfers wouldn't be able to surf the waves because of the generators.
   - (b) People think it would be too much of an eyesore.
   - (c) The animals would no longer be able to swim in the sea.
   - (d) Scientists worry it would generate too much noise and harm the animals.

   > **Think!**
   > Some answers are downright silly. Read paragraph 5 and look for the keywords *wave power*.

2. If you walk or ride a bike to school rather than getting someone to drive you, how are you helping the environment?
   - (a) I would be getting regular exercise.
   - (b) I would be helping to reduce fossil fuels being burned and reducing the amount of greenhouse gases.
   - (c) I would be able to help save money on gas.
   - (d) I would get a chance to spend time in the fresh air.

   > **Think!**
   > All the answers are true, but the question relates specifically to the environment.

3. If countries follow the Kyoto Agreement, what will be the possible outcome?

   _____

   _____

   _____

   > **Think!**
   > What is the *Kyoto Agreement* all about? Read paragraph 4.

4. What do scientists debate is the exact cause of global warming?

   _____

   _____

   _____

   > **Think!**
   > Look for the keywords *debate*, *exact cause*, and *global warming* in paragraph 1. Then read on to find the answer.

5. What does the writer think the effect of finding a solution to global warming will be?

   _____

   _____

   _____

   > **Think!**
   > Find keywords in paragraph 7.

Name _____

Use the strategies you have been practicing to help you identify cause and effect.

1. What would cause coastal cities to flood?

   (a) too much rainfall

   (b) people leaving their faucets running

   (c) all the extra storms that would be happening because of global warming

   (d) higher temperatures causing the water to expand and sea ice to melt

2. What would be the effects of more droughts for farmers?

   (a) There would be less water to bathe in and drink.

   (b) Crops would be difficult to grow, causing a food shortage.

   (c) We would have water restrictions and wouldn't be able to water our lawns.

   (d) Cooler environments would become warmer.

3. Explain some possible effects of global warming.

   _____

   _____

   _____

   _____

   _____

4. Explain what would happen if more people tried to do their part for the environment.

   _____

   _____

5. What is the cause of some people complaining about wind power?

   (a) They think it costs too much money.

   (b) They think the wind turbines are too tall.

   (c) They think the wind turbines spoil the scenery.

   (d) They think the wind turbines make it windier.

Cause and Effect

Name _____

Activity: Read the letter below and complete page 96.

Letter to the Principal

October 24

Dear Principal Wood,

   The student council would like to put forward a proposal to make our school "environmentally aware." We believe this would benefit all students in our school as well as the local environment. We have calculated that our school produces about 30 tons of trash each year—that's a lot! We think the school should work together in the following ways:

1. **Recycling**

   By supplying each classroom with two different-colored bins, students can easily sort recyclable trash. This would reduce the amount of trash the city would need to collect.

   General school trash can be recycled by labeling our wheeled bins as *glass*, *plastic*, *aluminium*, and *paper* and moving them into a central area.

   Some paper could be made into new paper by the third-grade and fifth-grade students as a joint project. The newly made paper could be used by art students to make holiday or birthday cards to sell as a fundraiser for the school.

2. **Worm farm**

   We can set up a school worm farm between buildings. The fifth-grade and the sixth-grade students could work together to maintain it. We could use some of the food scraps, cardboard, paper, and bark to further reduce our waste. The castings from the worm farm could be used by the school gardener to improve the soil.

3. **Compost**

   We could have a special bin for food scraps, which can be made into compost. By placing the bin near the lunch area during recess and lunch, students can empty their food scraps into it. Any clippings from the garden could also be added to make the compost, which can then be used to improve the soil and make the plants healthier.

4. **The no-packaging lunch box**

   We also think it would be a good idea to encourage students to reduce the amount of packaging they bring to school in their lunch boxes. We could have a class competition to calculate which class had the least amount of packaging in their lunch boxes, and they could win a class prize.

5. **Waste officers**

   To make things run smoothly, we think it would be a good idea to have a "waste officer" in each class. It would be that person's job to make sure electricity isn't wasted and recycling is happening in his or her class. This could reduce the electricity costs for our school.

   We hope you take the time to think about our ideas. It would mean spending some money on new resources to begin with, but it would be money well spent, and our environment would certainly benefit.

Kind regards,

The Student Council

Name _____

Use the strategies you learned and practiced in *Global Warming* to help you identify cause and effect.

> ## Remember:
> - A cause leads to an effect, and they are connected.
> - You will be told one, and you will need to determine the other.
> - Look for keywords in the question and underline them.
> - Find words in the text that are connected to the keywords.
> - Always check all possible answers before making a decision.

1. What would be the effect of the no-packaging lunch box idea?

   (a) Children would eat healthier foods.

   (b) Classes would win a special award.

   (c) There would be a reduction in the amount of trash brought to school.

   (d) There would be more trash to recycle.

> **Think!**
> Think about how it would help the environment.

2. What would cause the school garden soil to improve?

   (a) watering the garden longer

   (b) adding worm castings and compost to the garden

   (c) adding clippings to the garden

   (d) keeping the garden free of trash

3. Explain the possible effects of creating compost.

   _____

   _____

   _____

4. (a) What effect does the student council want to achieve by writing this letter?

   _____

   _____

   _____

   (b) Do you agree with the student council?   ○ Yes   ○ No

   (c) Describe the effect this letter had on you.

   _____

   _____

Fact or Opinion

Name _____

When reading, it is important to understand the difference between facts and opinions and to be able to determine which is which. A fact is something that is true. An opinion is something that someone *believes* is true.

Activity: Read the letter below and complete pages 98–100.

Letter to the Editor

Dear Editor,

1.   I read your article last month in *National Insectopia* where you totally vilified spiders. I've truly had enough of being made out to be the bad guy every time. It's been happening for ages, and it's not fair. Yeah, I look scary and I have hairy legs, but I'm not that bad! Just because Miss Muffet is a scaredy cat, everyone else thinks I'm scary, too.

2.   Really, people, take a look at yourselves. How huge are you compared to little old me? H-U-G-E! I should be scared of you, not the other way around. I know some of us can grow as large as a dinner plate, but most of us are pretty small compared to humans. Most spiders are harmless, you know, and if you leave us in peace, we'll quite happily go about our own business and leave you to yours. I know, everyone thinks our venom is deadly and all that, and I have to agree, some spiders are venomous and are quite nasty, but not me, and that goes for most of us.

3.   So many times, I'm in the garden minding my own business and I hear, "Mommy, come and look at the pretty spider!" At first I think that finally someone appreciates my beauty, then I realize I have to scurry for my life because here comes Mom with a broomstick to swipe at me! A quiet afternoon turns into a horror movie as I run for my life and watch my beautiful web being destroyed. All my hard work down the drain yet again! You people have no respect for another's property, and quite frankly I'm disappointed. Even if I make it inside your home, I don't go around breaking down walls and smashing windows. All I ask is that you give me the same courtesy as I give you. I know sometimes it can be a bit of a surprise if I turn up somewhere unexpected, but I'm really not trying to upset you—I just get a little lost occasionally.

4.   You know, we were one of the first animals to live on Earth, and we have been around for at least 400 million years—that's even before there were dinosaurs! Our life span isn't that long, so it would be great if you could just leave us alone to enjoy the time we have here, rather than making it a constant battle. Those beautiful webs you keep breaking down, because you think they look unsightly, are our specialized weapons for catching our prey and keeping all the insects around your house under control. We work for ages building our webs, spinning the silk and designing the trap. We spend long, quiet hours waiting for our prey so that we can wrap them in our silk and suck their bodily juices later—yum! Every time you get sick of seeing our webs and take to them with your broom, we have to start all over again. Do you have any idea how frustrating that can be for a humble spider like me?

5.   As if we don't have enough to contend with—being eaten by birds, lizards, and even other spiders—we really don't need to be under constant attack by you humans, too! Not all of us make it to adulthood; it's a perilous life for a spider. We aren't asking for special treatment—just to be left alone to get on with making webs and catching and eating prey. I promise, if you let us get on with our jobs, you'll have fewer insects inside your home—and surely that would make you happy.

Sincerely yours,

Stanley Spider

Name _____

Follow the steps below to learn how you can determine if something is a fact or an opinion.

- Ask yourself:

  Can the statement be checked and proven to be correct? If it can, it is a fact.

  Is it what someone *thinks* is true and can't be proven? If so, it is an opinion.

  > For example: Hens lay eggs. (fact)
  >
  > Eggs taste good. (opinion)

- Always check all possible answers before making a decision.

---

1. Which of these states an opinion?

   (a) Spiders have hairy legs.

   (b) The life span of spiders is shorter than that of humans.

   (c) You totally vilified spiders.

   (d) Some spiders can grow as large as a dinner plate.

2. Choose the best answer. Think about each choice carefully.

   (a) This is a fact that could easily be checked in books about spiders or on the Internet, so it is not the best answer.

   (b) This is a factual statement because the life span of a spider would be recorded anywhere there is information about spiders. This is not a good answer.

   (c) The article may well have vilified spiders, but the statement is someone's personal opinion about the article. This would be a very good answer, but you need to check all your choices.

   (d) The size spiders grow would be recorded and able to be checked wherever there is information on spiders. This is not the best answer.

1. Which sentence has both a fact and an opinion?

   (a) Only a few of us actually make it to adulthood.

   (b) Yeah, I look scary and I have hairy legs.

   (c) You people have no respect for another's property.

   (d) Just because Miss Muffet is a scaredy cat, everyone else thinks I'm scary, too.

2. Choose the best answer. Think about each choice carefully.

   (a) This is a fact and can be checked. There is no opinion in this sentence. This is not the right answer.

   (b) The fact in this sentence is "I have hairy legs," the rest is an opinion. This is probably the correct answer, but check all answers before making a decision.

   (c) This entire sentence is an opinion, so this is not the correct answer.

   (d) This sentence is an opinion, so this would not be the correct answer.

Fact or Opinion

Name _____

Use the strategies you learned to practice identifying facts and opinions. Use the clues in the "Think!" boxes to help you.

1. Which statement is an opinion?
    - (a) You keep breaking down our beautiful webs.
    - (b) Most spiders are harmless.
    - (c) Spiders can be eaten by other spiders.
    - (d) A spider wraps its prey in silk and sucks out its bodily juices later.

    > **Think!**
    > Which statement can't really be checked in factual resources?

2. Read the sentence from the text, and write one fact and one opinion.

    Not all of us make it to adulthood; it's a perilous life for a spider.

    Fact: _____

    _____

    Opinion: _____

    _____

    > **Think!**
    > There is one fact and one opinion. Write each as a sentence.

3. Read this sentence from the text.

    You know, we were some of the first animals to live on Earth and have been around for at least 400 million years.

    - (a) This sentence is ... ☐ a fact.   ☐ an opinion.
    - (b) Explain why you think this.

    _____

    _____

    _____

    > **Think!**
    > A fact is something that can be proven to be true. Find the sentence in the text and think about it.

4. Which sentence has both a fact and an opinion?
    - (a) Spiders can be prey to birds.
    - (b) Spiders try not to upset people.
    - (c) Everybody thinks spiders are scary.
    - (d) Some spiders are venomous and are quite nasty.

    > **Think!**
    > Which sentences contain facts, which contain opinions, and which one has both?

Name _____

Use the strategies you have been practicing to help you determine fact or opinion.

1. Which sentence is a fact?
   (a) Spiders are made out to be bad guys.
   (b) Spiders are small compared to humans.
   (c) Spiders often have days that turn into horror movies.
   (d) Spider webs are unsightly.

2. Which sentence is **not** a fact?
   (a) Spiders make webs.
   (b) Spiders use their webs for catching prey.
   (c) Spiders have been around since before the dinosaurs.
   (d) Spiders keep all insects under control.

3. (a) Is this sentence from the text ... ☐ a fact or ☐ an opinion?
   Just because Miss Muffet is a scaredy cat, everyone else thinks I'm scary, too.
   (b) Explain your answer.

   _____

   _____

   _____

4. Read the sentence from the text, and write one fact and one opinion.
   I promise, if you let us get on with our jobs, you'll have fewer insects inside your home—and surely that would make you happy!

   Fact: _____

   _____

   Opinion: _____

   _____

5. Which statement is an opinion?
   (a) Spiders can be killed by broomsticks.
   (b) Spiders' webs can be destroyed by humans.
   (c) Spiders think building webs is hard work.
   (d) Spiders can surprise you.

Name _____

Activity: Read the newspaper article below and complete page 102.

Fight for BMX Track Continues

Local residents and kids come to blows again over the proposed BMX track for Wilmington Park.

There were heated moments between the elderly residents of Wilmington Park Nursing Home and local teenagers this afternoon as the two groups collided over the city of Wilmington Park's proposal to build a BMX track for the youth of the community.

"It seems that the city has forgotten about our needs and only thinks about the kids in our community!" Mr. Jeeves explained. "I can't even catch a bus to town any more because of city cutbacks in the local transportation system, and here it is spending our taxpayers' money willy-nilly on people who don't even pay taxes!"

"Quite frankly, I've had enough!" cited Mrs. Ardro. "The city proposes to locate this BMX park right behind my unit. The noise of kids riding their bikes on the track at all hours of the day and night will be unbearable! At my age, I shouldn't have to put up with it!"

Not all the elderly residents of Wilmington Park Nursing Home feel this strongly—in fact, some strongly support the proposal.

"I actually think it is about time the city gave the youth somewhere they can go and blow off steam," stated Mr. Rush. "Maybe they will be less destructive if they have a place of their own. It will also encourage the kids to get some exercise! Kids need to get out into the fresh air and exercise."

The teenagers feel strongly about the BMX project and have been involved in the planning and layout of the track.

"I don't know why the oldies are so aggro about it. We are going to have set rules, and no one is allowed on the track after 6 p.m. in winter and 7:30 p.m. in summer—so we won't be riding our bikes at all hours of the night," said Misha Brown.

The kids of Wilmington Park community are planning a series of "busy bee" weekends to clear the area before construction begins.

"We felt it was important to help save the city money. That way, the city can spend the money on other things, too," stated Josh. "We really want to make the BMX track our own and intend to look after it!"

The local youth of Wilmington Park petitioned the city over five years ago with a proposal for a BMX track. The city has only just come to the party in recent months.

"It was a matter of calculating the costs and ensuring its viability," stated Mrs. Robinson, city representative for Wilmington Park. "We thought it would be a good idea to provide a place where they could go and have fun, and most importantly, get some exercise and fresh air. We are really proud of this project and have invested a great deal of time and effort into working with the kids to develop a BMX track that will be of benefit to the youth of Wilmington Park for many years to come."

The parents of the local youth are behind the park 100 percent and congratulate the city for working so closely with their children to get the project off the ground.

"I am Josh's dad, and I am so proud of him," stated Mr. William. "He has worked cooperatively with other kids to pursue this idea and to get the city to agree. We plan to support the kids in any way we can and intend to be there for the 'busy bees' to show them how proud we are of them."

Article by *Dee Sharp,*
Kids Issues

Name _____

Use the strategies you learned and practiced in *Letter to the Editor* to help you distinguish between facts and opinions.

Remember:
- Ask yourself:
  Can the statement be checked and proven to be correct? If it can, it is a fact.
  Is it what someone *thinks* is true and can't be proven? If so, it is an opinion.
- Always check all possible answers before making a decision.

---

1. Which sentence states an opinion?
   (a)   The teenagers have been involved in planning the track.
   (b)   The city has made cutbacks to the local transportation system.
   (c)   Maybe they will be less destructive if they have a place of their own.
   (d)   The new BMX track will be behind Mrs. Ardro's unit.

   Think!
   Facts can be checked; opinions can't. Which statement tells what someone thinks?

2. Read the sentence from the text and write two short sentences, one with a fact and one with an opinion.

   "I am Josh's dad, and I am so proud of him."

   Fact: _____

   _____

   Opinion: _____

   _____

3. Which statement is ***not*** an opinion?
   (a)   At my age, I shouldn't have to put up with it!
   (b)   The kids of Wilmington Park community are planning a series of "busy bee" weekends.
   (c)   We are really proud of this project.
   (d)   They are spending our taxpayers' money willy-nilly on people who don't even pay taxes!

4. (a)   Write one fact from the report.

   _____

   _____

   _____

   (b)   What is your opinion about the proposed BMX track?

   _____

   _____

   _____

   _____

5. Read this sentence from the text.
   The local youth of Wilmington Park petitioned the city over five years ago with a proposal for a BMX track.

   (a)   The information in this sentence is . . .
   [ ] a fact.   [ ] an opinion.

   (b)   Explain your answer.

   _____

   _____

   _____

   _____

Name _____

When we read, we should try to think like the writer to figure out how and what he or she feels and believes about the subject (point of view) and why he or she wrote the text (purpose).

Activity: Read the diary entries below and complete pages 104–106.

Too Much TV!

November 30

Everywhere I turn, people are telling me I watch too much TV, spend too much time on the computer, and play too many video games! But I like it! I like to get lost in the story lines, be absorbed in other people's lives, and escape my own boring life!

Mom is always telling me to read a good book. She read books when she was young and found the story lines totally absorbing and entertaining. I find books boring; it's too much hard work reading, especially when I can rent a DVD from the video store and watch a story in color. She gave me a copy of her favorite book of all time, *The Lion, the Witch and the Wardrobe*, and made me promise to read it for 30 minutes each day. She swears I won't be able to put it down—we'll see about that. When I have finished reading it, she has promised to rent the movie for me to watch. She thinks I will be able to see that the movie isn't always as good as the book!

My grandpa is always at me to learn a new game. He thinks of himself as a bit of a chess champion and wants me to spend one hour each week with him so he can teach me the game. He says it's better than any video game—whatever! Mom thinks I will really enjoy it, and it will help me to get to know my grandpa better. I'm not so sure about that; he's pretty old and boring!

Heather, my best friend at school, is starting to play basketball. Her mom and dad are making her play a sport because they think she spends too much time watching TV! It means Heather and I have to give up our computer chat because she will be at basketball practice. Heather wants me to play, too—that way we can chat face to face! I'm not so sure we'll really get time to chat while we are playing. Mom thinks it would be a good idea to play a sport, and it would mean Heather and I could spend some time together! I suppose that makes sense.

All these extra things to do; I don't know how I'm going to find the time to watch all my favorite shows. Dad says all I have to do is plan my time better, but I think it's all just a ploy to get me away from the TV and the computer.

January 25

Well, I got onto the Internet and did some of my own research about watching too much TV. I couldn't believe it! I didn't know that my generation is the least active of all time and it's causing huge health problems. They say we are heavier than previous generations of kids and at risk of heart disease and diabetes! I always thought old people got those diseases.

Luckily I had already decided to give my mom and grandpa some of my time to try out their ideas. I know it's not really active to read books and play games, but I truly think I've gotten smarter. I actually use my brain more, especially playing chess. Grandpa has been teaching me all about strategy and forward planning—really interesting stuff! We also have a chance to talk about his life when he was my age. He spent all his waking time outside on the farm with his dad, working with the animals and tending to the family crops. He thinks he was fitter than most of the kids today—he's probably right, too!

Mom was right about the book. I hate it when she's right! I couldn't put it down—I even found myself sneaking a flashlight under the blankets to finish a chapter some nights. What a fantastic story! My imagination was working overtime!! The movie doesn't even compare to the book; I was actually a bit disappointed. They left out some parts and changed others—I guess to fit in with the time frame of the movie.

I'm also really enjoying basketball with Heather. We even catch up two afternoons each week to go for a run and practice our ball skills at each other's houses. I think our friendship is even better than before. The coach gives great advice on getting fit and eating the right foods.

Dad asked me the other day how things were going with me. For once I could say, "Really good, Dad" instead of just moaning at him!

I'm feeling great, and I don't feel like my life is so boring! I don't actually need so much TV!

Name _____

Follow the steps below to learn how to identify the writer's point of view and his or her probable purpose or reason for writing the text.

- Writers don't always just tell you what they think or believe or why they have written the text. Sometimes, you have to try to think like they do and form a conclusion based on the information you've read.
- In the text, there are details and information related to the question for you to find, underline, and use in making your choices.
- Always consider all possible answers before making a decision.

1. The writer probably wrote the first diary entry because she:

   (a) wanted to make changes in her life, and by writing them down, she would be forced to follow through.

   (b) was bored of watching TV shows and playing video games.

   (c) hates writing diary entries.

   (d) wanted to express her frustration about the situation of the people around her wanting her to do more than watch TV, play video games, and spend time on the computer.

2. Choose the best answer. Think about each choice carefully.

   (a) The writer made it quite clear that she was happy the way things were. This is not the best answer.

   (b) She fills her time with TV, video games, and using the computer, so she doesn't get bored. This is not the best answer.

   (c) The writer seems to be quite good at writing in her diary. She probably would not have written it at all if she hates writing diary entries. This would not be the best answer.

   (d) Keeping a diary is a way of expressing your feelings; this is what the writer has done. This would be the best answer.

1. In the first diary entry, the writer believes that:

   (a) what happens on TV is better than what happens in her own life.

   (b) her grandpa is a really interesting person.

   (c) books are great to read and better than watching a DVD.

   (d) spending time exercising is better than playing computer games.

2. Choose the best answer. Think about each choice carefully.

   (a) The first paragraph talks about using TV as an escape that allows her to get absorbed in other people's lives. This is a good answer, but check all of them before making a decision.

   (b) She actually considered her grandpa to be old and boring in the first diary entry. This is not the best answer.

   (c) It is the writer's mother who thinks books are great to read and better than watching a DVD. This would not be the best answer.

   (d) The writer believes that exercising would take time away from her computer games. This is not the best answer.

Name _____

Use the strategies you learned to practice identifying what the writer believes about the subject and why he or she wrote the text. Use the clues in the "Think!" boxes to help you.

1. (a) Explain how the writer's relationship with Heather has changed from the first diary entry to the second.

    _____

    _____

    _____

    Think!
    Read both paragraphs involving Heather and compare the two.

    (b) What does the writer think about the changes?

    _____

    _____

    _____

2. What is the writer's point of view about books in the second diary entry?

    (a) She thinks books are boring.

    (b) She prefers to watch DVDs.

    (c) She thinks books are a good use of her imagination.

    (d) She thinks books are too much hard work to read.

    Think!
    Read both paragraphs involving books to find the clues you need.

3. What was her mother's purpose in encouraging the writer to learn chess from her grandpa?

    _____

    _____

    _____

    Think!
    Read the last sentence of the third paragraph.

4. Explain your own point of view about the writer's Internet research in the first paragraph of the second diary entry.

    _____

    _____

    _____

    _____

    _____

    Think!
    In what ways do you agree or disagree with the writer?

Name _____

Use the strategies you have been practicing to help you identify the writer's point of view and purpose.

1. What does the writer think about playing chess with her grandpa?

   (a) She was excited from the beginning to be spending more time with her grandpa.

   (b) She didn't want to at first but ended up liking the strategy and forward planning skills.

   (c) She didn't want to at first and still doesn't like it.

   (d) She asked her grandpa to teach her chess, so she was obviously interested.

2. Which sentence would the writer most likely disagree with now?

   (a) Go out and get involved in life, and then you don't need to watch so much TV.

   (b) Playing a sport helps to strengthen friendships.

   (c) Books are great for getting the imagination working.

   (d) Chess is a really boring game for old people.

3. (a) Think of four words you could use to describe the writer.

   I think the writer is . . .

   _____   _____

   _____   _____

   (b) Explain why you think this (your point of view).

   _____

   _____

   _____

4. The writer said, "I like to get lost in the story lines, be absorbed in other people's lives, and escape my own boring life!"

   (a) How did her attitude change after she made the changes to her life?

   _____

   _____

   (b) Do you think her attitude changed for the better?   ◯ Yes   ◯ No
       Explain.

   _____

   _____

5. What was her mother's purpose in encouraging the writer to read her favorite book?

   (a) to convince her daughter that movies are better than books

   (b) to reduce the amount of time her daughter spent watching TV

   (c) so her daughter would trust her opinions

   (d) so her daughter would get to know her grandfather

Name _____

Activity: Read the letter below and complete page 108.

Apology Letter

Dear Red,

1.   I am writing to apologize for nearly eating your grandma. My mom found out what I've been up to lately (apparently your grandma told her how badly I've been behaving), and she told me I have to write apology letters to everyone I have upset over the last month and explain my actions. I have nine letters to write, so it's going to take me a while to get around to everyone.

2.   My mom told me that it's not very nice to eat people's grandmas. She said that people love their grandmas, and you would have been very sad if your grandma hadn't been rescued. Mom said you would have missed all her hugs and kisses. I guess I never really thought about it that way. I never knew my grandma, so I don't really understand the bond you must have with her. It was the only way I could think of to get close to you. I often see you walking through the woods to your grandma's house and admire your slender legs and wonder how they would taste. Such young, juicy flesh would be divine and a well-earned break from eating the same old boring animals I eat all the time. Surely you can understand that I was just looking for a change in my menu.

3.   I've been on a bit of a rampage lately. I tricked the shepherd and his dog when I put on the sheepskin, hid among the sheep, and ate some of the lambs. Mom said that was a really mean thing to do. She said that the mother sheep would be very sad without their lambs. I've just been really hungry lately, and the little lambs looked absolutely scrumptious. Mom says I must be having a growth spurt and my body is telling me to eat more; but it's not acceptable to go around eating people OR lambs. I really didn't mean to upset anyone—I just don't know what to do!

4.   Even when I'm not causing trouble, everyone automatically thinks I am. I was hanging around the local watering hole just for something to do the other day, and everyone ran away screaming for their lives. I truly wasn't going to cause any trouble. I actually went down there because I thought it might be a good place to meet some friends. No one understands! I find being a wolf very lonely—I am generally quite shy and find it difficult to make friends. It makes it all the more difficult to find friends when all the stories show me as the bad guy—I know I do some stuff I shouldn't—but it would be nice to be the hero every now and then. I think I could be a great hero if given the chance; I have strong, powerful limbs for leaping to people's rescue!

5.   I don't have many friends and no one to really talk to about my feelings. Mom tries to be there for me, but it's just not the same as having a real friend. I can't talk to Mom about everything like I could if I had a best friend. The thing is that no one will want to be my friend if I keep behaving the way I do, so I have decided to turn over a new leaf. I am going to be more thoughtful and considerate of others and try really hard not to eat them! I am going to work hard to make some new friends, so I hope you accept my apology and that all will be forgiven. I am truly going to try to be a better wolf from now on!

Sincerely yours,

Wolfie

Name _____

Use the strategies you learned and practiced in *Too Much TV!* to help you identify the writer's point of view and purpose.

> ## Remember:
> • Writers don't always just tell you what they think or believe or why they have written the text. Sometimes, you have to try to think like they do and form this conclusion based on what you've read.
> • In the text, there are details and information related to the question for you to find and use in making your choices for each question. (These could be underlined.)
> • Consider all possible answers before making a decision.

1. Do you think Wolfie's reasons for nearly eating Grandma were okay? ◯ Yes ◯ No
   Explain.

   _____

   _____

   _____

> ## Think!
> Are you able to empathize with the writer?

2. What would be the best reason why Wolfie's mother made him write this letter?
   (a) She wanted Wolfie to practice his spelling.
   (b) She wanted Wolfie to be accountable for his actions.
   (c) She wanted Wolfie to make friends so he wouldn't be lonely.
   (d) She wanted Wolfie to sit and complete a quiet activity.

3. How does Wolfie feel about being the villain all the time?
   (a) He never thinks about it because it doesn't bother him one way or the other.
   (b) He would like to be a hero every now and then.
   (c) He thinks being a villain is a full-time job and works hard to be really good at it.
   (d) Everyone around him likes it when he is a villain and so does he.

4. Do you think the wolf was sincere in his apology? ◯ Yes ◯ No
   Explain.

   _____

   _____

   _____

5. What is your point of view about Wolfie's behavior?

   _____

   _____

Name _____

Activity: Read the passage below, and use pages 110–112 to show how well you can identify cause and effect, fact or opinion, and point of view and purpose.

Tropical Rainforests

1. Tropical rainforests are found in warm climates with heavy rainfall, sometimes as much as 2.5 cm each day. They are found in Australia, Asia, Central and South America, and Africa, in the belt that lies between the Tropic of Capricorn and the Tropic of Cancer. Tropical rainforests would have to be the most beautiful biome on the planet.

2. Tropical rainforests are home to more than half of the world's plant and animal species, including many endangered species. They are the most biologically diverse biomes on the planet. The stunning plants and remarkable animals that live in the rainforest have evolved over millions of years and have developed ways of working together to benefit and help each other. This is known as a *symbiotic relationship.*

3. Many different species of animals call the tropical rainforest, with its unique climate and habitat, home. The climate helps to provide plenty of food for the animals living there; the habitat is actually many different types of habitats within one. The canopy and the forest floor are very different and attract diverse types of animals, providing plenty of opportunity for various species to thrive.

4. The plants that have evolved and adapted to the rainforest environment are amazing—they are responsible for producing 40 percent of Earth's oxygen and stabilizing the climate on the planet. The plants absorb carbon dioxide, and therefore help to reduce the amount of this gas in the atmosphere. Through transpiration, the rainforests also contribute to the balance of the water cycle. They are responsible for adding water to the atmosphere, which then falls back to Earth as rainfall—without this process, more drought would occur. One-quarter of all medicines that we use to save lives and improve our health come from rainforest plants. The contribution made by rainforest plants to food and medicine cannot be matched by the plants in any other biome on the planet.

5. Only a few thousand years ago, tropical rainforests covered about 12 percent of Earth's land surface. Today, tropical rainforests cover only 2 percent of Earth's land surface. Around 80,000 acres of rainforest disappear each day, while another 80,000 acres are degraded beyond use by land clearing. The extremely destructive practice of logging is clearing rainforests. Timber is a highly sought-after commodity used in the building of homes and furniture as well as for firewood. Farmers clear the land for agriculture to grow crops or raise cattle, while large areas of rainforests are also cleared to make way for roads and major highways to improve accessibility to remote areas.

6. The problem with all this rainforest destruction is that less rainforest areas means more problems for Earth. When the tropical rainforests are destroyed, fewer trees convert carbon dioxide into oxygen. That means there is a build-up of carbon dioxide in the atmosphere, which contributes to global warming. Fewer trees means less transpiration, which means less rainfall, which contributes to the serious issue of drought. This impacts the entire planet by altering climatic conditions around the world. Fewer trees also means fewer roots holding the soil together. As a result, erosion increases and makes the land useless. The soil sometimes ends up in the river system, altering water levels and impacting the habitat of water life. Fewer tropical rainforests often means the extinction of plants and animals. In many instances, animals need to find new homes and are unable to survive in their new surroundings when having to compete for food and a home with unfamiliar species.

7. It is imperative for the survival of our planet to find a way to stop the destruction of such large areas of our most beautiful and hard-working biome on the planet—the tropical rainforest.

Name _____

> **Remember:**
> - A cause leads to an effect, and they are connected.
> - You will be told one, and you will need to identify the other.
> - Look for keywords in the question and underline them.
> - Find words in the text that are connected to the keywords.
> - Check all possible answers before making a decision.

1. What happens to the tropical rainforest when land is cleared for agriculture or to raise cattle?

(a) The rainforest plants grow even bigger.

(b) The rainforest animals stay behind to live with the cattle.

(c) The rainforest is destroyed, which leads to problems for the planet.

(d) Erosion occurs, which helps the farmers when planting crops.

2. Without rainforest plants, we would have:

(a) more oxygen in the atmosphere.

(b) to find alternative medicines to help us when we are sick.

(c) less drought and more rain.

(d) plenty of open spaces for rainforest animals to live.

3. What effect do rainforests have on the water cycle?

_____

_____

_____

4. What is the cause of rainforests having diverse types of animals?

_____

_____

_____

5. Large areas of rainforests are cleared to make way for roads and highways. What effect does this have on humans?

_____

_____

_____

6. What is the cause of some animals being unable to survive in new surroundings when their rainforest home is destroyed?

_____

_____

Fact or Opinion

Name _____

> **Remember:**
> - A fact can be checked and proven to be correct.
> - An opinion is what someone *believes* to be true, but it can't be proven.
> - Always check all possible answers before making a decision.

1. Which sentence states an opinion?

   (a) Through transpiration, the rainforests also contribute to the balance of the water cycle.

   (b) This impacts the entire planet by altering climatic conditions around the world.

   (c) As a result, erosion increases and makes the land useless.

   (d) Tropical rainforests would have to be the most beautiful biome on the planet.

2. Which sentence is a fact?

   (a) Tropical rainforests would have to be the most beautiful biome on the planet.

   (b) It is the most biologically diverse biome on the planet.

   (c) The plants in the rainforest are stunning.

   (d) The animals in the rainforest are remarkable.

3. Which sentence is *not* an opinion?

   (a) Tropical rainforests are beautiful.

   (b) Animals and plants in a tropical rainforest have a symbiotic relationship.

   (c) The plants in a tropical rainforest are stunning.

   (d) The rainforest biome is the most precious biome on the planet.

4. Read this sentence from the text.

   The contribution made by rainforest plants to food and medicine cannot be matched by the plants in any other biome on the planet.

   This sentence is . . . ☐ a fact.   ☐ an opinion.

   Explain why you think this.

   _____

   _____

5. Write one fact and one opinion from this sentence from the text.

   The plants that have evolved and adapted to the rainforest environment are amazing—they are responsible for producing 40 percent of Earth's oxygen and stabilizing the climate on the planet.

   Fact: _____

   _____

   Opinion: _____

   _____

Name _____

> **Remember:**
> - Writers don't always tell you what they believe—you may have to form a conclusion based on what you've read.
> - There are details and information you can find, underline, and use to help you to do this.
> - Always consider all possible answers before making a decision.

1. Most likely, why did the author write this report?

   (a) The writer wants people to keep destroying tropical rainforests.

   (b) The writer is a farmer and wants to explain why it is important to clear the land.

   (c) The writer wants to inform people of the importance of tropical rainforests to our planet.

   (d) The writer wants people to visit a tropical rainforest.

2. Which sentence would the author probably disagree with?

   (a) Rainforests help to balance the climatic conditions on our planet.

   (b) It is important to reduce global warming.

   (c) It is important that industry keeps logging to make the economy strong.

   (d) Rainforest plants are important for our survival.

3. The author would probably like to see:

   (a) the animals in the rainforests moved to the zoo for protection.

   (b) the tropical rainforests be saved.

   (c) the tropical rainforest plants grown in nurseries and sold to the public.

   (d) global warming increase.

4. (a) Think of four words to describe a tropical rainforest.

   I think a tropical rainforest is . . .

   _____   _____

   _____   _____

   (b) Explain.

   _____

   _____

5. (a) Do you think the author has a great appreciation for tropical rainforests?

   ◯ Yes   ◯ No

   (b) Explain why you think this.

   _____

   _____